I Promise To Keep Quiet
(After I'm Dead)

by

Lea Hope Becker

authorHOUSE®

AuthorHouse™
1663 Liberty Drive, Suite 200
Bloomington, IN 47403
www.authorhouse.com
Phone: 1-800-839-8640

ISBN: 978-1-4389-1949-2 (sc)

Printed in the United States of America
Bloomington, Indiana
This book is printed on acid-free paper.

This book is dedicated to my beloved and never forgotten parents. Without their extraordinary efforts to turn me into a mentsh, together with their supercharged gene pool, I would be drifting aimlessly as a passionless geezerette for the remainder of my days.

Contents

I PROMISE I WILL BE QUIET (AFTER I'M DEAD)

Maybe you saw the cover of this book on a shelf in a bookstore, and opened it, thinking it was the story of a former lady gangster with secrets to reveal -- or possibly the ruminations of a partially recovered escapee from a nut house. Well, tough luck, it's not. That book you are holding in your hand is just something I decided to write to get some old garbage off my mind. I'm not going to glorify it any more than that. I just happen to be an outspoken schnook raised by a pair of other outspoken schnooks, residents of an average neighborhood of nobodies, most of whose lives were pretty boring.

So why buy this book? I'm no celebrity -- I'm not even a genius or a compulsive gambler -- although I am compulsive. There are two simple reasons why I wrote it:

(1) Now that I'm a seventy-one year old lady, I can finally tell the truth about my undiagnosed insanity because all the other principal players in my personal drama are dead. I also thought it might be a good idea to put some of my childhood anecdotes in book form, rather than have them buried in some sort of time capsule. Knowing my history, nobody I know would ever dig it up anyway.

(2) The second reason is that I need your money. I want you to purchase this relatively cheap book as a charitable contribution to my personal fund, and, trust me -- it's not even tax deductible.

I'll let you in on a little secret -- I had a third reason. They say senior citizens who want to avoid memory loss should exercise their brains more. So by having to write in sentence form, in halfway decent English, I'm doing it. I am taking my brain out for a walk.

I'm a survivor, I think. Yes, indeed, I've just checked my pulse. After living through a tumultuous childhood, crisis-filled puberty, interrupted schooling, multiple marriages, childbirth, divorce, career revisions (I've even practiced law for thirty years), health issues and a few other bumps in the road, it's time for me to be able to let go of pretense and face reality. (Yiikes!)

Actually, I hate facing reality. It gives me the itches and takes me on that wild ride back into my past. All those memories are still vivid. When I was a four-year-old tomboy, I had a lack of well-behaved mentors to guide me. I was an only child until age eight of two working parents living in a storefront neighborhood where the only kids my age were rowdy little boys who were always dirty and played mean. I probably thought I was supposed to act like the little devils that they were.

Fortunately, this stage of my young life ran its course and I settled down to a relatively calm existence as a mere rebel. I never got over that stage, but I'm harmless enough.

I like the idea of starting a new project at age seventy-one, so I'm ready to reduce my craziness and compulsive behavior to a few chapters of light reading. I have tried hard to keep it light because my attitude is, if you want to get into something heavy, you're better off reading one of William Shakespeare's tragedies. I've had fun doing this project, so maybe you'll chuckle a little bit as you follow some of my antics. If you don't, well then, I've still got your money.

I have come to the conclusion that it's a mistake to take the road of life too seriously, so I simply view it as a scenic bypass carved out of the murky human jungle.

CHAPTER ONE
THE TRUTH ABOUT MY
CAREER PATH
(You may call it a "Vocation" if you wish -- feel free)

This is one of the very few pictures taken of me recently where my smile didn't come out all funny. I thought I might need a smiling picture of me some day if I ever did something even a little bit serious.

So here goes -- I'm about to launch into a quickie review of how I got to be that person in the photo -- that's about as serious as I can get.

* * * *

At the time I was born during FDR's second term in the year 1937, newborn girls of Jewish families were clucked over as though each of them was destined to be a future Queen of America, deserving of tiaras and velvet pillows. This was a lot of B/S because Americans never crowned any royal heads, at least not literally. I learned that all the initial excitement over my birth was part of a gigantic plot to fool little girl children into thinking that life would be beautiful. The whole thing -- all the adulation -- was just a ploy. As an infant, I never acquired a single tiara or velvet pillow -- only a few lousy pink rattles and a rash.

You have to understand my culture -- the ooh and aah crowd of Jewish drumbeaters in the late thirties. Some of them still thought that the next Queen Esther was just around the corner. We were expected to turn out gorgeous and highly skilled at homemaking and motherhood. If we were funny-looking, we still could be prettied up with nice clothes, nose jobs and cute hair styles, but then our credentials as homemakers and potential mothers had to be superb. There's a Yiddish term for what a young girl was supposed to become -- it is pronounced "balabuste." I have learned that Yiddish terms are spelled many different ways. It is characteristic of me that I didn't realize that earlier in my life -- I learned it last week. Oh well, let me get on with it.

We didn't acquire most of these "balabuste" credentials in school -- we got them from heavy-handed mothering. My own high school, where the percentage of Jewish girls was quite high, threw in a few "Domestic Happiness" classes as electives. I know what I'm talking about because I am looking at my high school yearbook while I am writing this. There, in that noteworthy record of my high school life, are pictures of my female classmates modeling dresses they had sewn and displaying cookies which they had baked. When Hilary Rodham Clinton made her well-publicized remark about baking cookies, I knew exactly what she was talking about, even though she is younger than I am, as are most people.

I didn't sign up for any of these domesticity classes because I had other plans. However, it is interesting to note that I was in the pictures anyway. It has something to do with the fact that I was the Editor of the high school yearbook, and I pretty much had things my own way. The supervising teacher who was supposed to be guiding me was either on sick leave some of the time, or else she just trusted me to be editorially honest. When the pictures were taken, I must have sat in on many of them, because there is my face, smiling as though I had just been indoctrinated as a future model housewife.

When each of us had to submit our ten-year ambition in a few words for the individual yearbook picture, I counted up the girls in my 206-person high school class who wanted to be "homemakers" a/k/a "happily married" as a vocation. There were seventy who admitted to it in print. I was one of the seventy, although I had included the term "married" as the third career. My first choice was "famous syndicated columnist," second was "author" and bringing up the rear was "wife." The year was 1954.

Jewish girls born in the late thirties tended to be named after an ancestor named either Mildred, Becky or Sylvia. Becky was usually a nickname for Rebecca. However, tradition allowed parents to use just the first letter for a more modern-sounding name. The names Marilyn, Barbara or Sandra appeared to win out over Mildred, Becky or Sylvia. I referred again to our yearbook and we didn't have a single Mildred or Becky and only one Sylvia. But there were six Marilyns, six Barbaras and five Sandras.

Maybe some ace at research can discover how many Jewish jokes there are about women named Mildred, Becky or Sylvia, but I guarantee there are only a few such jokes with women named Marilyn. (Is it possible that fewer Jewish jokes have been created in more modern times?) I'm not sure how our given first names may have influenced our lives, but since I was named Leah, after a great-grandmother I never knew, I was one of the few young ladies given a first name that is more common today than it once was. That's interesting. Some people acquainted with me think that I am more common than I used to be. I assumed that my great-grandmother, Leah, was a decent soul, because my mother wanted only the best kind of life for me.

Shortly after my birth, I was given a nickname which my mother and two of her best friends quickly attached to me, and it stuck. I'm keeping it out of this expose. I was content to let people call me anything they liked until I turned fifteen. Then, one of my teachers suggested that my use of the nickname, which was admittedly cutesy-poo, was undignified, and didn't I want people to call me by my given name? I thought about his suggestion seriously, but as long as everyone was going to have to get accustomed to calling me by my given name, Leah, I had a singular opportunity to do something rebellious, so I dropped the "h" and began using the name spelling I have today -- Lea. My reasoning was that the "h" was a silent letter, and there wasn't anything silent about me.

My mother was descended from a long line of sufferers, and I suspect that the suffering syndrome was passed down through the female line. Many of our people became affluent sufferers, being a highly motivated group. Of the seventy female graduates in my class who wanted to be married, according to the yearbook, no fewer than thirty mentioned that they wanted to be married to money. It's right there in print -- flat out. When I think about it, it seems like a pretty good idea, especially nowadays.

A few girls, besides me, mentioned specific careers they desired, but having attended three class reunions and also having kept up with the gossip during recent get-togethers, I have learned that hardly any of them actually remained in their yearbook-specified vocation and many of these career aspirers never had a career outside the home and family at all. It is my guess, and I'm probably close to being right about this, that nearly all my female classmates got married within three years of high school graduation. Many of these marriages are still going strong today, so I guess our 1936-37 crop of newborns didn't get sucked into the divorce maelstrom later on as is the case with couples today. The cause behind this statistic has probably been the subject of somebody else's book. As I'm pondering this particular fact, I would expect there are dozens of such books out there.

I am married, happily, for the third time, and I am about to embark on the career which I named as second choice in my yearbook -- author. It's probably too late for me to become a "famous syndicated columnist," but if one of the current publications is interested in hiring me, I'm still available.

I just pulled out my most recent resume, for purposes of whoever might be interested in my trail of accomplishments, and it seems to portray a person who couldn't bear to be pinned down to only one job or vocation. Therefore, the truth about my vocation is that I am multi-vocational. I have no clue as to why my resume has gotten longer and longer, while my income has gotten smaller and smaller. This imbalance is not what my third finance teacher in my second college would have anticipated.

Oh, I have to add another vocational note: The following piece of my history never got into the yearbook: I had lots of ephemeral career goals as a young girl, but I once seriously thought I should have become an astronomer because I spent so much time staring into space. Mom would shout to me, "What in the world are you doing in the bathroom so long?" I would answer back in an audible shriek, "I'm thinking about tomorrow!" Then Mom would shrilly come back with, "Well, pick up the stuff in your room today, or you won't even be breathing tomorrow!" This was a heady threat, but whether or not I picked up my stuff, she let me live another day.

If I was weak in my desire to deal with the clutter in my room, it was because I was very much absorbed in thinking about the Sun, the Moon and the Stars. I had a book given to me on the subject, and I wondered what it would feel like to be peering through the great telescope at Mount Wilson. The problem I had was that I had no proven math skills, no good habits of study, no dedication to any one area of education and no mentors in my family to encourage me except one aunt who sometimes worked as a secretary for the Government. When she had time to kill, she tried to teach me things, and I did learn a lot of Geography and Shakespeare from her, but it did not appear to increase my sense of self-worth. Maybe that's because when I would recite some verse or spell difficult words at the age of three, my mother and her lady friends always said that it was "cute." Nobody, not even my employed aunt, treated me as a budding genius. I certainly couldn't figure out my destiny, so I just went along, rather rebelliously, with the rules of the road and pursued the path of least resistance. In my family, that path meant being a "good" girl, a balabuste, and probably not an astronomy student.

I've dealt seriously with my identity crisis, and can say with all honesty, that today I know exactly who I am, especially when I go through my piles and piles of memorabilia. However, I have never really looked like the teeny picture on my driver's license nor the intensely Photoshopped portrait of me recently printed by my husband. I thought I looked younger than my age in it, and asked him, "Honey, did you do anything to that picture? I think I look pretty good in it!" He answered, "I had to leave in a few of the wrinkles because I didn't want the picture to look phony." That was tactful, wasn't it?

So that's about it. I'm about to spew forth some of my heartfelt offerings with some of the wrinkles left in. I wouldn't want to be phony in my writing any more than in my photographs.

CHAPTER TWO
THE GRITTY TRUTH ABOUT
MY CHILDHOOD

A Not So Short Chapter, Formatted To Fit Your Short Attention Span

I don't know why some babies are born with placid personalities and others are born as little monsters. I had a reputation as being a fussy child, always wailing and demanding. Some people have hinted

that I was born with a silver spoon in my mouth, so maybe that had something to do with it -- you know -- tarnish and all that toxic metal. I never slept at night and kept my folks awake so much that they began to have bad dreams, which included visualizations of floors soaked with vomit and urine. They both had the same dreams. I didn't drive them crazy, however, because they were already crazy. My fussiness weighed heavily on my mother to such an extent that she became afraid to take care of me. So she decided to get help and hired a series of baby-sitters of questionable credentials whom she did not interview carefully. If I didn't turn out right with this arrangement, well, there was always good old-fashioned discipline. It went something like this: "Just wait 'til your father comes home!"

Mom was really a career woman at heart, but she didn't know it. Otherwise, why did she have to make all sorts of excuses to avoid caring for me as a little baby? I wouldn't have blamed her. Nevertheless, she created one big all-encompassing all-occasion excuse so she wouldn't have to keep devising new schemes. She found a job as an assistant to my father in his packaged liquor business. He almost didn't hire her because he wanted a wife to come home to. How could she be in both places? But her salary request was too favorable for Daddy to turn down. She was perfectly willing to work for no pay and to cheerfully turn over the day's receipts to him. This meant that she would have less time to go clothes or furniture shopping. For Daddy, it was a win-win situation.

I didn't mind being left in the care of baby-sitters -- I rather preferred it because each sitter always started out trying to be nice to me. We had a huge sitter turnover, however, so I developed a great memory at aged two, just learning all the different names and which name went with which personality and peculiarity. For instance, we had one baby-sitter who would get homesick the minute she came over to watch me, so we had to go to her house. I secretly think she developed claustrophobia trying to manage tying my shoelaces while I was sitting on my parents' full-sized bed. It was a room that was 10 feet by 9 feet. In it was a full bedroom set of carved maple, an easy chair for my dad to sit on when he needed to put on his shoes and socks, two floor lamps, a baby crib, a nightstand, two narrow extra chests for my mother's scarves, unwanted gifts and balled-up rayon hose, and an antique-looking grandfather's clock. It was fake.

I loved my homesick, claustrophobic baby-sitter's house because it had so many rooms. You couldn't even see most of the rooms when you came in through the front entrance, because the doors to the downstairs rooms were closed to keep their dog out of the front hall. He had a habit of jumping on visitors and licking their necks and ears and everything else he could get to. One of these days I'm going to get a memory flash and recall the name of that dog. I know it wasn't "Fido." There were rickety stairs to a second floor. Everything in that house was old, including the floorboards. They creaked when someone walked on them, even me. I probably weighed about thirty-five pounds. In the living room there was a very old rocking chair which never stopped rocking, even when no one was on it. I couldn't figure that one out. But the best room in the house was my baby-sitter's room on the second floor. It was so bright and airy, and at least twice the size of my parents' bedroom and contained less furniture. I didn't see a bed in the room, so I figured it would be hidden in a closet, like the one my grandma had in her dining room. Then I learned that the bed where she slept was in still another room on the second floor. The room which I thought was the bedroom was really called a playroom. I decided then and there, and I was still a pre-schooler, that claustrophobia was caused by apartment living and made up my mind that when I grew up I was never going to catch it.

MARY'S BIG HOUSE

My baby-sitter's name was Mary, and she was a fanatical movie buff. Instead of framed oil paintings of bowls of flowers on her playroom walls, which I thought were mandatory for walls where people lived, she had pasted all over them full-page pictures of her favorite movie stars which she had torn out of movie magazines. If I'd have known it was OK to do that, I'd have had a ball tearing up our Look magazines. She taught me all about movie stars and her favorite female star was Priscilla Lane. Mary had four full page torn-out pictures of Priscilla Lane on the wall and in each of them the star looked amazing. My mother certainly never looked anything like that.

I hated when it was time to go home. I was extremely jealous of Mary and of her big old house and her collection of movie magazines. However, I had discovered a whole new world out there which was larger and brighter and had more space than I had ever dreamed people could inhabit. Our four-room apartment at home had only one level and two narrow, deep closets. Each of the closets was filled with mothballs. I never saw a moth, but my mother was afraid there might be one some day and she didn't want any holes in her sweaters. This puzzled me because she didn't own any sweaters. I only saw her in her nightgown when she woke up and her coat when she left the house. What she was wearing under the coat was completely left to my imagination.

I could go on and on about all the things I loved about my movie-star-loving baby-sitter's house, but my favorite part was the lure of whatever was on the upper floors. That house not only had squeaky stairs to a second floor, but it had an enormous attic on top of that second floor and another flight of stairs up to that attic. There were lots of valuable things in that attic, but I was not allowed to venture past the top stair -- I could only look at some of the contents while Mary had me leashed to her hand. I guess my mother had told her I was a bit wild. That wasn't fair. Just because I used to rearrange all the living room furniture while mother was away at work does not mean that I couldn't be trusted. I guess the last straw was when I decided that her new Chinese porcelain lamp looked better in the neighbors' apartment, so I gave it to them.

I had another baby-sitter who also left an impression on me, but she either wasn't homesick or didn't have a house because she slept over and was supposed to cook meals. My mother kept Kosher, so she explained to the baby sitter about keeping the dishes and pots all separate. The baby-sitter couldn't remember all the instructions, so when Mom found out that I was eating cookies made with milk off the meat platter and cheese dumplings sautéed in chicken fat, she just lost it. It was the first time I ever saw my grown-up mother cry. She must have impetuously made up her mind to stay home and take care of me because I remember finally seeing my mother wearing a dress. It had flowers printed all over it and was referred to as a "house dress." I guess that meant she was only supposed to wear it indoors, but I had no way of knowing whether she ever wore it under her coat and went outside with it because her experiment at staying home only lasted a short time. My dad had gotten used to my mom being his loyal employee and they got along better when she wasn't shopping or complaining about my behavior.

Back I went to be cared for by good old reliable Mary at her terrific house almost every day. I must have really felt that I was part of her family because I started to think that their dog was my dog. I loved that friendly dog and hugged and kissed it a lot, but felt very sad that I couldn't take it home with me. I figured Mary's folks were somewhat possessive, so I stopped asking.

Mary's family stored food differently than mine did. My mom used to keep all the cans and cereal boxes in cabinets that were too high for me to reach and in a pantry that I couldn't get in because the white-painted door was always stuck, so I had to wait until an adult got some food for me. That's the one thing I really appreciated about my parents -- without them I'd surely have starved. Mary's kitchen was much more child-friendly because there were lots of cabinets out in the open and on the bottom and they were filled with canned food and lots of boxes of other goodies. One day when they weren't looking I opened a box of dry cereal and started eating pieces of it. I thought it tasted better than anything that we had at my house. Mary's mother started to laugh when she discovered me and said I had gotten into the dog's food. I still don't understand why I thought it tasted so good. Maybe my mother was bad at picking out cereal.

For me, life was just one disappointment after another. Every day of my young life seemed to include some kind of crisis. My parents were always wailing about a bunch of problems, but the worst was about not having enough money and the second worst was my mother's cooking. It seems she couldn't get my father's thick steaks well done enough. He apparently wanted them so hard that they would bounce off the plate. That confused me, because if we were so poor, why didn't mother make more meals with hash as the main course? The tumult in my family had its effect on me, and I kept thinking up ways to arrange for my parents to move out -- maybe to another country. Of course, they would first have to get the pantry door fixed.

Throughout the entire ruckus, and in spite of it, I finally reached school age. I figured it would be a big opportunity for me to turn the corner. I was badly mistaken. Nobody liked me, not even the teacher. I had never learned how to get along with other kids my age, so I always said the wrong thing. I did it on purpose. If another little girl asked me if I wanted to play with her, I would say that I didn't know any girl games and that I had to keep my outfit perfectly clean because my mother didn't have a good routine for doing laundry. I thought it would be more fun to play with the little boys anyway, but our playground supervisors wouldn't let me use their equipment and the boys just wanted to pull my pigtails. I tried to defend myself by kicking the perpetrators and shrieking as loudly as possible, but the playground supervisor made me stop. I didn't understand boys or girls of my age, so I just played by myself.

I guess you could say that I did not get off to a good start socially. However, I did become adept at day-dreaming and making up stories. Some of the stories were gruesome, but I destroyed these quickly. Even I did not want to read them. I didn't want any nightmares of my own making. Then I wrote silly stories and those I did read. I don't have any of my silly stories today, but I did write and save rather catchy little jingles which I thought I would show to my friends -- that is, if I ever made any. I did not think I was well-behaved or smart or likeable, so I reacted accordingly. I became a problem child. Incidentally, it is nearly impossible to write down all this serious stuff without feeling some remorse, so the next part of this tale is being written with the aid of some mind-numbing pills I have somewhere.

Being a problem child was not easy. It was difficult to keep thinking up new escapades, but I managed. One way I could get attention was to aggravate my mother with behavior she hated. If she would bake a cake for dad and the two of us, I would get to the cake first and eat most of it. When I went to school, I kept losing my jackets and other accessories. That got my mother's attention a lot because she couldn't let me go to school without a wrap on chilly days or she would worry that I would catch a bad cold. I never caught a really serious cold, but I did enjoy seeing her displaying her guilt by wringing her hands nervously. Mom was an extremely accomplished worrier and an even more accomplished nagger. I used to observe her nagging my dad for things, and it almost always worked, so I copied her nagging technique and acquired a huge collection of coloring books, dolls and doll clothing and building blocks.

Having a nearly non-existent social life meant I had a great deal of time to develop the type of personal skills which did not require playmates. I became adept at fashions from performing constant dolly wardrobe changes. This was before Barbie, but that didn't matter to me, since I had lots of reference material. There were cut-out books, picture books, coloring books, and Childrens' Activities© books. I read everything in sight and used my newfound knowledge to develop verbal and visual mastery. I suppose my mother kept buying me stuff to keep me occupied, and it must have worked out, because she appeared to have survived my early years with scarcely any damage -- except maybe a few extra headaches. OK, it was a lot of extra headaches.

My mother used to annoy me with tales of her upbringing during the Great Depression. I wasn't very tactful, so I would run out of the room and hide somewhere whenever I suspected that a lecture was happening. Since our two closets stunk of mothballs, I had to crawl under the furniture wherever I could fit. I remember doing this because I occasionally had dreams of being imprisoned by metal springs. Mother also seemed to enjoy telling me the usual kiddie lies -- how hard she and Daddy sacrificed to give me the things I wanted, and how ungrateful I was. Sometimes she went on and on about this issue during our many visits to the toy store. I learned to tune her out and concentrate on the loot I was getting.

My early memories of my father had to do with his running his cocktail lounge with a liquor store attached. Maybe it was the other way around. I think the liquor store came first and then, to stuff even more money in one of those registers they had then, he put in a cocktail lounge. I wasn't allowed to hang out in there much because of my tender years. My mom wasn't crazy about being there either. She kept complaining that she didn't like to have anything to do with the drunken bums that came there, but she went anyway. Mother was very practical. She could always get away from the drunken bums, but she had to live with my father. She didn't always get to do what was fun for her.

Other memories I have of my dad had to do with his card playing and his yelling. He was a short man with a huge voice. He probably should have been an opera singer, but instead he spent most of his time mixing highballs. They probably didn't have aptitude tests when he was raised, and even if they did, his family had too many kids to notice him. He loved playing cards with his men friends. I was allowed to watch them play if I kept my mouth shut. I watched them so often that I learned the game of gin rummy before I was good at brushing my teeth or washing my face. Nobody in my family had their priorities straight.

I know that I preferred the activities of boys more than the activities of girls because what the boys did wasn't as boring. They used to run and jump more and were allowed to climb trees and leap across buildings. I tried to imitate them and got scolded because it wasn't ladylike. This ladylike thing had me perplexed. I could never understand it because it always seemed like my father had so much more fun than my mother. He giggled a lot more, and she would get embarrassed whenever he giggled too loudly. But the poor guy was having a good time -- didn't that count? I still feel that way today, even though mother outlived him by thirty years. Daddy had a sense of humor when he wasn't yelling or drunk, while my mother was usually cranky. Come to think of it, my father had a sense of humor even when he was drunk. All my mother's friends felt sorry for her because my father was such a loudmouth and had such a volatile temper. I felt sorry for my mother because she had to be ladylike. The most ladylike quality she had was her ability to nag with real spirit. Any time she felt deprived she knew exactly how to get her way by expressing herself. Her ladylike voice really wasn't that muted. I could hear my parents yelling in the house when I was playing outside, even down the block. The whole neighborhood knew about our finances. They also knew I wasn't a model child. Little did they know that I would grow up to be a closet cynic with hearing problems.

I couldn't help but admire my mother for hanging in there during my father's bad moods. My admiration for my mother's courage reached an all-time high when, in spite of our explosive relationship while I was in the third grade at school, she decided to have another child. Did she think there was safety in numbers? I don't know. But this time she made a decision to be a stay-at-home mother. My father changed businesses and now didn't need her hanging around his new enterprise. I figured that the secret to business success meant you could fire your wife. So my mom got pregnant. She hoped this child would be a boy. What a mistake! She actually had one. He was not the answer to her prayers. But I was happy. Now she had another human being to pick on to give me some relief. I thought he was kind of cute in a smelly sort of way. As soon as he learned to talk, he dispensed with words such as da-da and ma-ma. His first word was "No." Actually, that's the only word he really spoke for a long time, so I had to frame my questions carefully. I would ask him, "Do you <u>mind</u> if I carry you around the house like a puppy?" The predictable answer gave me permission to do what I wanted with him.

We became the best of friends and now I had a playmate who was my virtual prisoner. I was eight years older than him, so I was the boss. I read to him those stories that I liked. My favorite ones were monster and horror stories. At first I stuck to my versions of Red Riding Hood and Hansel and Gretel. I changed the endings. Red Riding Hood did not survive being eaten by the wolf and Hansel and Gretel's bread crumb trail disappeared and they both died in the woods. Then, as my reading ability improved, I graduated to tales by Edgar Allan Poe. My little brother was lucky to have me around. He learned how to be naughty from my mother, however. The game they played went like so: She would straighten up the kitchen and clean the floor and everything, and then he would mess it all up so she had to do it all over again. I think there was a method to my mother's madness. There were no workout gyms for stay-at-home mothers in those days, so that's how she got her exercise.

We had moved from our small apartment to a fairly large house with a large kitchen. The cabinets were now upper and lower. They were easy to open by a baby with curiosity. Soon all the carefully arranged canned goods were rolling around the floor. My parents called my brother a "holy terror," but I don't think there was anything holy about him. He was just another brat. These were not quite the good old days. My brother and I would have turned out better if we had grown up on a farm where we had some responsibility, but the economy had grown to the point where our job as kids was to ruin any chance of having our parents save money. We had so many toys between us that if there really had been a Santa Claus, he would have scratched his head and gone on to the next chimney. Most of my brother's toys got broken quickly, but were even more quickly replaced with new toys so that he would not feel deprived. This fact might have something to do with my brother's going through a lot of cars and motorcycles because of his accidents in later life, but to get into that now would be counter-productive. Suffice it to say that the owners of all the toy stores we frequented got the best of the deal.

Anyone who has grown up in a household with battling parents like mine will understand what an ordeal it was. Those kids who didn't succumb to psychosis actually thrived. You simply ducked when you had to. On bad days a kid like me could wander out the front door and find an empty lot somewhere with a few trees. The more trees in the lot, the longer you could linger without being found. I was a bit of a child naturalist without realizing it. I spent quite a bit of time looking at leaves and bugs for as long as it took for my folks to get over whatever was eating them. Then I would casually arrive back at home like nothing ever happened. If my mom asked me where I had been, I told her I was looking for berries for a school science assignment. Mom was pretty naive, since I hardly ever did any homework. She was also in a constant state of distraction. Her mind was mostly on cooking, cleaning and explaining her latest purchases to my dad. I took advantage of her mercilessly. Eventually, I found out that she was onto me all the time, but figured things would change after I graduated from high school. Was she ever wrong! She had never reckoned that my dreams and ambitions came out of books she had never read. I think I was destined to be a misfit and a rebel, but I intended to have lots of fun in the process -- that is -- without getting into too much trouble. I was only a little bit of a devil.

As I matured into a thin-skinned teenager with hopes and dreams of a world beyond high school, I developed a philosophy of life in such a household. Get out. Soon I realized that my small allowance and some baby-sitting money I earned could be better spent on something other than clothes and make-up -- luggage. Although I plotted and planned for some way of escaping from those ear-splitting arguments, which I figured were common between husbands and wives of the fifties -- those couples who had become numb to the fact that nobody ever won -- I had difficulty seeing myself earning an honest living and maintaining my own place. After all, making my own bed in the morning was not one of my greater achievements. Why do housework when the Fairy Godmother went over my bedroom with a fine tooth comb every day while I was at school? I did have another option, however. I had been accepted to a good college, located in a suburb. At least I could escape some of the trauma while I was away at school. Also, I thought I could make some pin money writing skits and songs. I had written the Class Song for my high school graduation, adapting my own lyrics to a well-known tune. I felt so proud of myself and thought I might make a good lyricist if only I could get someone to write the music. What I didn't realize at the time was that even Rodgers and Hammerstein had to struggle against major odds before they came up with really great songs. I used to dream that everything would be so easy for me and that doors would just open up and light my way. All those movies I had seen as a kid made me starry-eyed, but my come-uppance was about to occur.

I learned the bad news just before I was to begin college. Yes, the hard truth hit me hard. Why does truth have to sting so much? I had visualized being a member of a sorority house on campus with friendly and chatty group study sessions and parties every weekend. It was not to be. There was no money available for me to live like a Queen on campus, not even for a year. Baby-sitting money and part-time jobs weren't going to cut it. I would have to invest my small savings in a good set of earplugs for surviving at home and fall back on commuting to the halls of higher learning. So I borrowed one of my dad's leftover autos from his high-on-the-hog days and drove to school on cheap gas. But I forgot to bring my good attitude and my aptitude for learning with me. Wouldn't you know it? I got caught up in ogling college boys wearing sweaters with Greek letters instead of absorbing mandatory lectures. No one told me about the hot pants problem. I proceeded to one of the bigger mistakes of my life. I went on a diet without getting good advice. I lost a lot of pounds and looked a lot sexier, but I must have cut out nourishing grub, because I could not sleep at night and kept catching up on my z's in class.

I'm skipping over the part about getting failing grades, dropping out and pretending it was all the fault of the school because I know today that I was already a nut case then. Without a college degree I had lost my excuse and my meal ticket for a pre-feminist existence living in my own digs.

Even as a youngster, I knew that I was being taught the wrong subjects at school. What good were three years of High School Latin going to do for me when what I needed was a course in Living Within Your Means? I had already learned the other lifestyle. I was trapped in a dilemma of major proportions. If I followed the pattern of other high school girls of my era, I would simply choose some male victim to have nuptials with and, after an appropriate interval called an engagement, followed by a wedding of great extravagance, a graceful exit from the parental homestead could be made. I didn't like the catch to that plan, however. The catch was the vows I would have to take. What I really desired was complete independence. Complete independence in those years for a non-degreed seventeen-year-old girl meant living poor. Unfortunately, I was not equipped to live as a hippie, since that concept had not been hatched yet. It was still the age of Bohemians. I was willing to try anything, at least for a week.

Being a Jewish Princess and living a Bohemian lifestyle was not one of my well-conceived plans in 1956. First of all, I didn't have any money to spend on the beauty parlor after dishing out my miniscule grocery store wages on carfare to get to the Bohemian hangouts. Also, I needed an outfit which would blend in with the local coffee house. It had to look worn out, as though I were a starving artist. I was neither an artist nor starving. But I did think I could pull off my scheme if I looked at least a little hungry. I went on a more sensible diet and stayed awake during the day. Then I could have energy to still be wild in the evening. I needed a buddy to give me courage, so I picked out one of my college dropout girlfriends who actually was artistic and poor. We were a pair. We were two Jewish girls mingling with unwashed oddball jocks over demitasse cups in a coffee house establishment behind on the rent. We waited until one of them invited us up to his loft to examine his etchings. The invitation came, but I don't remember actually making the visit. Maybe my friend did, but I froze up. I think I got on the next bus and went home to Mama. Oh boy, was I ever confused about my identity after that. And before that also.

My middle name is Hope, but I think it should have been Charity. I needed some. I was too honest to go into an illegal venture and too brainwashed to do something courageous, so I became a secretary. What a laugher. Me making coffee which I actually poured for someone else! The first time I had to pour coffee for a conference of only guys, I forgot to put the cup under the spout. Don't even ask. I became a whiz at typing, stenography, obedience, and all the rest of the usual secretarial skills. I pulled it off because my alternative was not good. I had seen too many Tennessee Williams movies about misfit women wearing torn dresses. So I behaved nicely for a couple of years until my mother's ideal prospective mate for me showed up. He was the perfect male victim and when he popped the question, I answered

"Yes." Whew. Now I had somebody of my very own to go into combat with on a daily basis.

Emulating my mother's role in marriage, I learned to cook and baked lots of cakes which I proceeded to eat whenever it was necessary. Occasionally my husband got to taste them -- if he was quick. I pretended to be happy and I was so good at it, I even believed my own pretense. For nine years I thought I was the ideal wife and mother of three. Who was kidding whom? Without realizing it, I was trying to become just like my mother. But underneath it all, something was fishy. If marriage didn't work well for her, how could it possibly work for me, a woman who could read, type and even had some college on my resume? Maybe I had picked out the wrong husband. I had long been a believer of that adage, "If at first you don't succeed, try, try again." I consulted the Yellow Pages under "Lawyers." That phase and grueling stage of life being completed, I went back to those same Yellow Pages and looked up "Psychiatrists." I was also a believer of that adage, "Better late than never." So I chose late quite early.

I went for mental health counseling. No, wait a moment -- I should have gone for mental health counseling. Instead I got married again. Then I went for mental health counseling. I guess I did things backwards. I went for a quick second marriage and then I thought about whether I should do it. At least I was accumulating some pretty flattering wedding pictures of me. I don't remember if I had money problems or the hot pants problem all over again. Actually, I had both. This gets worse.

I have to digress again and go back to my first marriage. I was such an unfulfilled wife that I had to invent a new addiction in order to escape from marital reality. I called it -- housecleaning. But I don't mean run-of-the-mill housecleaning. That type would have been normal. I became a germ-free, obsessed, maniacal, frenzied, ashtray-carrying, lunatic fanatic. I didn't wash the eating utensils -- I sterilized them. I would run the dishwasher several times with the same load, just to be sure. Then it occurred to me that I might be trying to compensate for some old dirt. After all, I had never moved the refrigerator since we moved into the house. Only God knew what was under that thing! I stifled my instinct to do the right thing and left the unknown grime undisturbed.

Then I turned my attention to the bedrooms. The beds didn't get made casually -- all the bedding had to be completely free of creases and wrinkles, even if I had to drag out the ironing board. The sheets had to be changed every day to suit my moods, so I bought all the colors there were. Black wasn't fashionable then -- stores didn't have that color -- so I had some custom-made. Then I started on the kitchen. It was a long, narrow room, hard to decorate, so I did what decorators did. I started with the best features -- two beautiful windows. I decided on awnings. I had them installed inside the room. You know, in case the roof leaked, they would protect against water damage. Then I went after the cabinets.

When we bought the house, all the built-in kitchen cabinets were varnished light wood. Varnish yellows with age, so they looked kind of yellow. But the alcove paneling was a pink-tinged ash wood. I hated the clash of woods, so I actually stripped all the cabinets. There were lots of cabinets. I hated that job, and it took forever, but it was better than spending time with you know who. Then I painted the cabinets bright lemon yellow and put on orange molding and ceramic hardware and decided I was a better carpenter and designer than a wife. The kitchen was now very bright and helped my mood when I had to cook in it. One of our guests said she had to put on sunglasses when she visited. I hated the original floor that was on it, so I changed that too. There was a new technique that involved pouring a new floor over the old one, which I promptly had installed. It didn't need waxing, they promised. They forgot to tell me about the smell. It was pretty toxic and may have affected my husband's thinking ability. As for me, it drove me almost sane.

I went on and redid the rest of the house and made everything brighter. I thought there was a happy person inside me -- somewhere. This happy person saw everything in yellow and orange.

I tried being religious and began to go back to my roots. Since I loved yellow and orange so much, I started with the Sun-God. It didn't help. I couldn't walk like an Egyptian. Too much of me was Jewish. I had been raised as a Jewish child in training to be a Jewish teenager. I remember those years. My father used to pray in synagogue. While he was praying, my mom was checking over my High Holiday outfit. I was on display, next to the other girls. I hate mentioning this, but I have to get it out in the open: My prayers were kept a secret. I prayed for a really hot guy. I should have prayed more out loud. Then, maybe, God would have heard.

My first marriage was so dull that I had to invent my own excitement. I bought a notepad and began to write down X-rated things that I was going to do, but I was so shy I was afraid to read what I wrote, so I tore everything up immediately. The other young wives had coffee klatches. But I was terrible at coffee klatches because I hated coffee. I wasn't really crazy about the young wives either. I was too indoctrinated with guilt to run away from home, so I stayed there -- but I read stories about Joan of Arc, Amelia Earhart and Annie Oakley. I wasn't brave, but I read brave. I watched TV a lot in those days. I loved Lucy. She divorced Desi, you know. It looked pretty easy, like all I needed to do was to get a little courage. I didn't get courage suddenly. It took several days. From my point of view, I was reaching out. From my friends' and relatives' point of view, I had flipped. They tried to advise me. I hated nosy people. I tried to be agreeable. As a form of therapy, I drew pictures of all the women who wanted to help me. I made them all look like Groucho Marx.

Nothing helped. So here I am -- your everyday neurotic. I discovered that I could never change my childhood -- just my attitude. Haste makes waste, of course. So, I'm waiting.

I have to go back in time again in order to make sense out of some things. They say that the first five years are the formative years of a child's life. Sometimes I think that in my case they were the deformative years. I know that I daydreamed a lot, but I think all kids daydream. I never took a poll at the time to determine how many kids daydreamed. I didn't know what a poll was because I don't think they were common in those days. If you had asked me then what a poll was, I would have answered that it was something tall that had to be avoided while riding a bike on the sidewalk.

My daydreams were about being a big shot. My father used that term a lot. I got it from him and thought it meant everyone would admire you. Oh how I wanted to be admired. People who were admired had lots of friends. I dreamed of being a movie actress. I don't think it was about the money -- I think it was about the fame and the great wardrobes female actresses wore. The first acting practice I indulged in as a kid was to look innocent when I knew I had done something naughty. With a great deal of effort, I developed a "who, me?" expression. It deceived no one. I had little talent for covering up my petty crimes.

My mother, in a different era, could have been a detective. Well, let me modify that -- she could have been a clumsy detective, such as the character in the "Pink Panther"© movies, Inspector Clousseau. She wasn't very good at solving problems, because she kept having more and more of her own, but boy, was she good at identification! She would have made a fabulous fingerprint technician. She could see a chocolatey pinkie impression on a newly polished table from the next room. Then there was her aptitude for accounting. She must have kept a meticulous inventory of the treats stored in her pantry, because she seemed to know exactly how much of the contents of a box of cookies or crackers had been extracted. She was also skilled at finding out if the packaging had been breached. Mom was born too early. In today's world she would have made a fabulous Quality Control expert.

I tried to use a different alibi each time I was caught misbehaving. Bad behavior on my part was met with the three S's -- Screaming, Scolding and Spanking. I would not have made a good politician because I never could master the required arts of diversion and persuasion. I wanted Mom to laugh at me and forget about the spanking, but she had too good a memory and too fragile a sense of humor. I got spanked often and learned all about guilt and defense mechanisms and first aid. You could call it Basic Training for little girls. When you sniffed that a fanny whacking was imminent and you were small and athletic, you ran like hell. I became an accomplished runner and darter. During this period I also acquired the kind of emotional survival skills that females have always needed, no matter what liberation philosophy prevailed -- the ability to cry at the drop of a hat and to scream for emphasis. All too soon I would need these skills for marriage.

I also received advanced training in being uprooted and learning the names of new playmates and neighbors. By the time I was eight years old, my family had moved us eight times. That didn't count visits to my grandma, where they would leave me for a few weeks at a time. They probably wished they didn't have to come back and get me. I knew that they had tried to ship me off to a boarding school when I was three, but they chickened out. I never knew if they changed their minds or if the boarding school people purposely upped the tuition after they met me and my parents.

After we had occupied several different apartments during the World War II years, we finally settled down in a neighborhood where I could meet kids my age, with the possibility of getting to know more than their names. Our next door neighbor lady who lived in the house just to the south of us seemed friendly and approachable. I don't remember every memory clearly, but I do happily recall that this smiley-faced Italian woman seemed to take an instant liking to me. We bonded quickly. Even after we had lived in different places after many years, I kept in touch with her. I remember that recently she told me that the day we moved in I went up to her and asked her, "Do you have any little girls for me to play with?" She thought it was so cute of me and told me she had two daughters, one a year younger than me and one three years younger. I was glad to settle for that situation. She remembered enjoying how happy I was to hear that good news. I do remember that I had no trouble getting to know these two girls and that we became really good friends. I spent a lot of time at their house until they had to send me home for dinner. I think that's when I began to redevelop a nose twitch which I had had as a toddler. I also believe it was about always being required to go home to the wild bunch.

The house just to the north of us had a son my age, but they were moving out a few months after we moved in, so I don't remember much about him, except that his name was Jerome and he was chubby and friendly. The people that bought his house were a married couple with four daughters, one of whom was my age. I took an instant dislike to the mother because she gave me her own nickname which I didn't like. She seemed bossy and nosy and had a shrill voice that almost never got turned off. Also, it seems she was the type who would tease me a lot. I didn't need teasing, I needed friendship and approval. Too bad I was such a polite kid, or I would have given her a mouth. None of her four daughters seemed easy to love either. I needed companionship, so I made the best of things. But oh, how I regretted the day that the four-daughter parental team took over the turf of the chubby boy.

I must have been a pretty unfulfilled youngster, because I closeted myself with books and yummy treats instead of being a social butterfly. Books and reading became my salvation and my favorite foods and snacks became my accompaniment when I read. Snacking went with reading and reading went with snacking. This combination became an entrenched habit. We didn't have a TV until I was eleven, but when it finally arrived on the scene, I was able to make the adjustment and snack while watching TV. But I never gave up refuge reading. Just when it seemed that I could get through a day, or even a few hours, without being intruded upon by mom or dad, just when I thought I could quietly engross myself with some enjoyable reading material while addictively chomping on something tasty, my mom got on my case. She had been doing her detective work and had been observing how much I ate, during mealtimes and otherwise. She said that I was getting a big tuchis. She painted a really grim picture about girls who were too fat. They couldn't look good in clothes and would get ridiculed in school. I wasn't really fat, but I did have a sizeable butt for my frame.

My memory tells me that mom started hocking me about my eating about the time I was in seventh grade. That's when my worst rebellion began. All my mother had to do was to warn me about what I shouldn't do. I took her guidance as something which required deft connivance to get around. However, I did become a worry wart about getting fat and began to devise my own ill-conceived diets. After a few weeks of being hungry, I had had enough and became a food sneak. I learned how to smuggle my favorite snacks into my room and eat them when no one was around. One of my very favorite snacks was a chunk of salami which I would slice off the bottom of a very long roll of this delectable sausage. Of course I had to find it first, because my mother had resorted to hiding certain foods. I always unearthed her hiding places, especially the location of the salami. How can anyone expect a young girl with a good nose like a doggie not to smell her way to the hidden cache? I used to store the chunk I had surreptitiously removed in one of my dresser drawers until I was ready to eat it. Eventually, my drawers began to smell like a delicatessen.

I became a little chubby, but somehow I never got really fat because I got a lot of exercise running around outside and bicycle riding. The best kind of running was the kind that got me as far from my parents as I could go without getting lost. That's why bike riding was so great. I could make a faster getaway.

We had physical education in school every day, and I soon realized that I was somewhat athletic. My athleticism wasn't the natural kind, however. I was athletic because I was so strongly motivated to outdo the other kids in sports. They had a system in physical education where two opposing leaders of a game, such as baseball, got to pick out the members of the team. I was never picked as the leader, probably because I was usually the shortest kid in the class. I won't even go into what it was like to be a shrimp in an ocean of piranhas. I needed to make a name for myself as being a great competitor. Nevertheless, I was nearly always the last kid picked when the leaders had to round out the team. Girl leaders were different from boy leaders, I guess. Boy leaders in gym class mostly picked team members who were good athletes. Girl leaders mostly picked team members based on what the kids looked like and whether they could be bullied. I had been told that my mother dressed me funny. I know I was bullied by these girls, and I blamed it on my inability to stand up for myself. How come I could stand up like a world champion fighter to my mother and sometimes my dad, while I cringed and quivered in the face of kids my own age? I chalk it up to lack of practice. I had spent too much time living in solitary.

As a student I had an opportunity to take advantage of my reading skills. I also was a great speller. I liked to do well in school because it made me feel better about myself. I started to make more friends at home, but in school there were few kids who chose playmates because they got better grades and knew more of the answers. The age of nerds had not arrived yet, at least not at my school. Everyone seemed dumb to me, but that's only because I got the best marks in the class. Since I was convinced I was hopelessly stupid, wasn't it logical to conclude that the rest of the class consisted of idiots? Since I never discussed these ideas with anyone at all, my thoughts were never confirmed. I had brainwashed myself into believing that I was an unattractive, unlovable, overweight klutz. The klutz part was probably correct. When I tried to sing out loud, people would shush me. When I tried to dance, everyone who saw me would laugh. When I spoke up, I would get teased and called by nicknames I hated. I don't remember being described as a pretty child. All I remember is that adults and children would feel sorry for me because I had to wear thick glasses and ugly shoes. Kids would taunt me because my socks were funny. What a life.

The girls in my neighborhood liked to play jump rope. I must have acted like a clown, because one of the four daughters next door to me -- the one who was in my grade at school -- told me years later that I used to turn the rope with my teeth. How come I don't remember doing this? Was she lying? I can't believe it really happened that way! I have kicked myself one hundred times for not cross-examining her to see if she was in error. It's too late now -- she's dead. She died of a heart attack at age 49. I went to her funeral, but I can't say I ever felt really close to her the way I would have wished. I hope God forgives me for thinking about some of her demeaning comments while I was sitting through the service. Maybe I did turn the rope with my teeth. Maybe I was a clown. Maybe I still am.

* * * *

I seem to get a lot of flashbacks as I cogitate about my past life. Do other people of my age get flashbacks so vivid that they seem like they had just occurred? I not only get visions of scenes and faces and dialogue, I seem to be able to bring back the emotions associated with these personal re-enactments. I do think of myself as a self-shrink. I not only experience an emotion embedded with a flashback, I concurrently hear myself asking me, "How do I feel about that?" And then I even answer myself. I get a certain smugness today when I compare my memory of feelings with those of my husband. For example, I'll ask him if he remembers his favorite games of childhood. His stock answer is, "I don't remember having a childhood." How can you reminisce with a man like that? Every interesting past experience I bring up gets responded to with a few syllables and a resumption of his reading the newspaper. I don't believe he really doesn't remember stuff. I think he is a reincarnation of some Buddha somewhere -- all wisdom and no weaknesses. His only weakness is having married me, which he apparently did in a fit of lust and wishful thinking. We made it work because we compromise so well -- we do things his way.

I'm never at a loss for words, so why do I lose words? Sometimes when I am talking about something, I will get a blank for a very important word, or often a name. They say this, uh, something, uh, condition, occurs with advancing age. It's supposed to be the beginning of the slowing up of brain functions. This is grossly unfair. When we get older we need our wits about us more than ever. I'm running out of excuses. I'm also running out of time to come up with new excuses. I'm beginning to dislike maturity, and I complain about that to my husband, but he tells me I have nothing to worry about.

Meanwhile, back at the flashbacks. Hey, that sounds silly -- back at the flashbacks. That's two times going backwards -- is that like a double negative? I mean, if you go back at the flashbacks, could that mean you are going forward? Why don't they have flash-forwards? I would love to look ahead. Then maybe I wouldn't lose so much money gambling on failing publicly held companies. Maybe I wouldn't throw out my old fashions which are soon to come back in style. Flash-forwards would be just great. I began to dwell on being able to flash forward so much that I decided to learn more about time and space. I even drove to Batavia, Illinois to visit Fermilab. I bought scientific books. Most of these books were about quarks and colliders. Then I discovered Stephen Hawking. He seemed to be an expert on time and space. I thought that maybe he could help me, so I bought his books. I kept reading and re-reading them, but I had trouble digesting some of the theories. I tried reading these books while eating a cookie, but it didn't help. Scientist talk is so off the chart for me that I am happy if I understand that the universe is a big something. That's right. There's something out there. So I keep trying to flash forward. I'll let you know when I'm able to digest tomorrow's newspaper today.

I've let myself digress. I'm supposed to be describing the Truth about my Childhood ad nauseum. It's important to me to be able to understand my childhood so that I can finish it. I really want to move on.

I don't really feel that I can tell the entire truth about my past because it would involve some sexuality thoughts. My mother taught me that little girls weren't supposed to know anything at all. It was for their own good. I never made head or tail out of that advice. How can a human being be better off by shutting out knowledge? Look at what's happening in schools today: Kids learn about the details of procreation before they learn certain difficult words and concepts, like "work" or "pay bills." If I had a great-grandchild, which I don't and probably won't, he or she would now be in school learning things I was taught that I shouldn't know. Is this why there is a so-called Generation Gap? I think it's a big problem. How could it be that failure to know sex stuff in my past means that I am out of touch and poorly equipped to give advice to people in my present? I did eventually learn about sex along the way and have some pretty good stories to prove it. However, I'm not planning to publicly reveal these stories because in my heart of hearts I feel that my mother was right about one thing -- it's none of your business.

Well, I got that part out of the way. Let's go on to other facets of life.

I am dying to discuss career choices for young ladies in the fifties. I'm talking about the 1950's, by the way, for those of you who believe that the modern age began with Paul McCartney. Before I graduated high school, we were given some career counseling. Somebody who counseled me must have mentioned a career in Journalism, because I decided to try it. I think I remember a scribble on my aptitude profile saying that I was nosy and outspoken. Career choices for young ladies in the fifties did include a few scarce jobs in the media, newspapers, magazines, advertising, gossip columns, etc., but I found out later they were mainly descriptions of college classes which were available. But don't get me wrong -- it was possible for a woman to land a job with a newspaper back then -- think of Lois Lane© -- but such a woman needed a certain personality. She had to have guts, moxie, intelligence, ambition, credentials, bravery, connections, creativity, willingness to learn, thick skin, all those qualities that Superman's© woman should embody, because he would have the keys to the executive washroom. I know I was badly advised to try that field -- back in the fifties -- because look at my own personality at the time: Instead of guts, I had self-doubt. Instead of moxie, I was a nail-biter. Instead of intelligence, I was carefully taught that I wasn't supposed to act too smart and that sex was something I shouldn't even ask about until the wedding night. Instead of ambition, I had daydreams which exploded like bubbles whenever I mentioned them. Instead of credentials, I was a dropout waiting to happen. Instead of bravery, I was a coward waiting for bedtime so I could bury my head in a pillow. Instead of connections, I had advice, such as, "Don't do that!" Instead of creativity, I had a mother who threw out my drawings because the outside of the refrigerator had to be polished every day. Instead of a willingness to learn, I had a willingness to fall asleep in class. Instead of thick skin, I had skinned knees and an inferiority complex.

I know I sound like I'm whining about the past. I know I'd like to make whining about the past a major field of education. I enjoy whining about the past because it takes my mind off the aging process, where, if you live long enough, you can acquire arthritis, rheumatism, backache and impotency. How can I enjoy any credibility when I tell young kids today to respect their elders, since I never listened to my mother? It's a total hypocrisy! I'm hopelessly caught up in conflict and culture clash. I was the anti-matter to my parents' matter. The reason I can still live with myself is that I silently enjoy being confused most of the time. Who wouldn't be if you listen enough to political candidates giving you straight talk? I'm also an optimist. When the world as we know it finally comes to an end in a pile of rubble, and if I'm still around, having taken even a small part of my mother's advice, I will have this crack to deliver: "Don't forget to wash your hands."

CHAPTER THREE
THE GRITTY TRUTH ABOUT
MY APPETITE

A muddled babble about my lifelong pondering about my weight
issues, regurgitated

I've been puzzled about many phenomena in this life, but the most puzzling thing that I have encountered is why girls wind up with such differently shaped bodies. There were always some skinny girls at my school, but the one I remember most was named Jackie. She was also very tall, so she not only towered over me -- she reminded me of a toothpick with some knobs here and there. I made friends with her because I wanted to know her secret. All I found out was that her parents nearly went broke trying to feed her several brothers, who were equally toothpicky and even taller, but that Jackie never had much of an appetite. I'll just refer to her as Miss Toothpick. There was also a very very plump gal whose picture wasn't even in our yearbook, so I guess she didn't graduate with us. I've forgotten her name altogether, but I'll refer to her as Miss Second Helping, because I do have a recollection of how she did lunch in our high school cafeteria.

Things were different for teen-aged girls in the fifties. Anyone who has seen the movie, "Grease," may not recall seeing any overweight girls in the cast. I don't remember seeing them, so maybe Hollywood had some kind of weight limit, like the airlines used to have. Do they still? Never mind. Anyway, I stored away in my bag of body rules that girls like Miss Toothpick had simply too much vertical mass to fill up and not much interest in culinary delights, whereas Miss Second Helping really appreciated the tastes and smells of our cafeteria offerings, which made her unique right there.

After years of intense study, mainly involving reading how-to books and then discussing the newfound knowledge with myself, usually in the shower, I have come to a conclusion that is far removed from astrological signs, Albert Einstein equations and Dr. Spock: The shapes of people can all be blamed on the pediatricians. They just don't come to the table with a full plate of parental understanding.

My first postulate has to do with the pediatrician that my mother hired after I had emerged from her body, upside down and squirming. Incidentally, I hear that nowadays dads are in the delivery room and some even take videos of the birth. In the days when my mother had me, they gave her some sort of doped up stuff and she was sent home to block the whole bloody mess out of her mind. It isn't just that times have changed -- it is just that I get so freaked out thinking about how all these young techies celebrate the birth of kids and then go home and find new ways to screw them all up. Am I wrong, or are more people mismanaging their kids' eating patterns today than ever? I look around me and I see more fat kids now than when I was a squirt. OK, OK, I shouldn't use the word "fat," but I can't help it. It's so roundly descriptive -- only three letters -- so perfectly tailored for people who no longer know how to spell. "Chubby" is not much better, but, hey, I grew up with the tact of the late thirties.

Well, back to my mother's choice of baby doctors -- he was old-fashioned as soon as he got out of medical school and then must have fallen behind in his Continuing Ed. I know for a fact that while he kept up with nutritional literature tailored to the mother's needs, his books and the medicine of the day didn't even include warnings! It is my belief that none of the boxes of Pablum had asterisked notations about the danger of feeding that stuff to an infant in a terrible mood.

I don't think any of the pediatricians in the thirties paid much attention to the parents' family histories. If our good doctor had done so, he would have unearthed the fact that I came from a long line of traditional cooks and also a long line of heart attack victims. I don't think there's a coincidence here. Did my mom's hired food expert with stethoscope attached and tongue depressor at the ready even think once whether my eating squished this and pulverized that would get me on the right path? Forget about today's gene science hoodoo, just for purposes of my argument. Forget about the fact that I have survived to let off steam into my seventies. Forget everything I have just said.

It's really OK with me that my ancestors and parents and even my pediatrician get to rest in peace while I sweat it out on a stationary bike and still read calorie charts. Despite all their misguided advice and lack of penetrating research, I forgive them. It's me that I haven't made nice with. I still fret that my frame looks like a cross between a shorter version of Miss Toothpick and a slightly thinner version of Miss Second Helping. My weight still fluctuates like the stock market does, although not nearly as much as when I was young, except that in my case I don't feel very good about the capital gains when it goes up. When my husband swears that he loves me "anyway," I think, what is this crapola word "anyway" anyway? I think it means that he accepts that I am still all screwed up about my eating habits, my vanity and my exercise routine. To paraphrase my favorite clown, Woody Allen, how can I respect a man who would settle for me as a wife?

So now, to the gritty part of the truth about my appetite, I begin with the saga of my relationship with food in my infancy.

I don't actually remember what I ate or how I ate as an infant. I remember kicking my little legs in a crib while lying on my back, but that's it. The rest is blank that early in my dear little life. However, I do have a pretty good idea what my pediatrician would have instructed my mother to feed me because when I had my first child I hired the same pediatrician! I figured that if I could survive his ingenuity, my daughter probably could too. It is almost a certainty that his infant feeding instructions would not have changed in 26 years because he did not believe in changing methods that still worked.

So I probably started on orange juice, then baby cereal, then squished fruit and then squished vegetables. Mushed-up meats would have started in about the fifth month of my life if I survived the transitional diet, which I did, because I'm right here telling about it. Mom said I got my first tooth at four months and that I stood up in my bed at six months. I don't think mother would have fibbed about these facts, so I guess I can rest assured that nobody thought there was anything "wrong." She also told me that I was colic-y and that I fussed an awful lot, and that she was always afraid that I was not nursing enough nor eating enough, so at about five months she stopped trying to nurse me and began to improvise. It's a cinch that this improvisation had some ominous consequences, because I have the cancelled checks paid to therapists and other experts to prove it.

I remember hot dogs at baseball games and lamb chops, where Mom would cut one up for me into very small pieces. She didn't trust me to use a serrated knife myself, even though I was capable of making a hammered copper ashtray that I learned how to do at school. I remember hating spinach and mom's inspired decision to mix them up into my mashed potatoes, which I did like. It was a good way to ruin perfectly delicious mashed potatoes, but she intimidated me with threats I can't remember. I didn't hate peas as much, and I almost liked corn. Cauliflower smelled funny and mom never bought cabbage because her mom never knew about cabbage. Mom did serve corned beef, however, and this came from a small delicatessen which also sold very red fat hot dogs. They were the best. I could have lived on them, if I had had my way. Dessert was good too, and I must admit, my mom served great desserts. Some were even home made. You got to eat a dessert if you ate your spinach, even if it was mashed in with your potato.

Do you see the backwards value system in the above account? If you eat your spinach, you get to have dessert? Does this blather still go on today? Is spinach so awful that you have to be bribed with sweet follow-ups that get some of us on the road to perverse dieting? Why didn't mom do it the other way? If you eat your dessert, I have some great spinach waiting for you? Would I have known the difference? Maybe I would have grown up like rabbits do -- or even better, like a skinny movie actress? Was mother on the phone with the pediatrician asking if it was OK to have to mash my spinach up with my potatoes? I will carry this resentment to my deathbed. When the final curtain is being ordered and my very last doctor asks me if I want something to make me more comfortable, I'm going to lambaste the entire medical profession and then tell him that yes, I want a plate of plain spinach. No potatoes please. My God, I need to get this stuff off my chest!

I do have a very vivid memory of having to eat cooked carrots. That's another thing I'm pissed off about. I'm pretty certain I was about four years old when my mother actually fed me her cooked carrots, one forkful at a time, which I would only eat if she told me a story. Why did I think that carrots were so awful that I had to be bribed to eat them? I eat carrots today -- they're not so bad. I sweeten them, put them in soup, immerse them in dressing-laden salad, chomp on them naked (I mean, the carrots, not me), and even have a liking for carrot cake, which I'm forbidden to eat by my food policeman, my husband. I think carrots should be enshrined as life-saving nourishment.

As this four-year-old bribee, however, I know that Mom told me that carrots were good for my eyes, but since my eyes became crossed at age three, and I had to wear glasses, why didn't she come to my rescue earlier? Didn't mom know that carrots were the answer to crossed eyes from the get go? Didn't she listen to the pediatrician at all? That's why I blame him -- he should have known better than to leave force-feeding and bribery up to my mother. Too late now -- I'm still wearing glasses, even though my eyes eventually stopped crossing. That still leaves open the problem about the mix-up in my head.

Mothers, if your child is a picky eater, don't give the kid anything but whatever baby Jackie Toothpick or a skinny movie actress got to eat. And if you have to get into stuff like breaking through family eating patterns and all that psychobabble, just remember that some day your kids will decide what to do with you when you are lying there in a hospital, sick as a dog.

I know that after two years of age I became a normal sized active little child because I have pictures. In one picture of me, I actually looked almost skinny. That must have driven my mother out of her mind because if a kid was skinny, it reflected on the family.

Family mealtimes were loud and rough talk was often exchanged between my parents. It wasn't always in English either. They spoke enough Yiddish to confuse me, but I could make out some of the words which described my table behavior, and it wasn't good news. I was a deceitful eater and messed around with the stuff on my plate which didn't appeal to me. I did love lamb chop bones, however, because my father kidded me that I left less meat on a rib bone than a hungry dog. I could never understand why nobody was interested in eating marrow from inside the bones, because it seemed OK to me. I might have even sucked some of it out if I was hungry enough. I'm being very frank. I wanted to have my own rules about food and about everything else because I had an extremely independent mind. If mother said one thing, I knew that the opposite of what she said would not only get her goat, but maybe even be a good idea.

Mom was at least twenty pounds overweight during my early childhood, so I know somehow she received nourishment when I wasn't looking. She never sat down at the table for dinner, since she was a hovering type of cook and serving lady. She had to check dad and me to see if the morsels were disappearing. Mom was extremely distrustful of people who were eating her cooking -- I think she was afraid that she might have shorted us on the size of the portions. Living through the Great Depression might have had its effect on her, but I know there were some mothers out there who occasionally looked at something other than their kids' plates of food -- just not mine.

I will never forget those meals of boiled chicken, overcooked vegetables, mashed potatoes and chicken soup with barley. Salad was a few pieces of lettuce adorned with a sliver of tomato and a dollop of sour cream. Mother served something called "Farmer's Chop Suey," but it didn't look anything like real Chop Suey, which we ate at a Chinese restaurant. Real Chop Suey was somewhat appealing, so long as I wasn't forced to eat Egg Foo Yung. I could have told those Chinese cooks how real pancakes should be made, because that's one thing my mom could really swing at, but I had to keep my mouth shut and be polite so my parents wouldn't be ashamed of me. It was useless because they were ashamed of me anyway.

The Goldilocks legend with the famous concept of not too hot, not too cold, but just right, infiltrated much of the wisdom of the times when I was emerging as a tuchis with a wardrobe. Too skinny was bad and too plump was worse. Just right meant that there would be no end to sons of rich fathers coming to call. Now who would quarrel with this basic truth in daughter-raising, either then or now? If this premise isn't true, then how would you interpret the following scene which is so emblazoned in my memory that even total brain dysfunction would still leave it intact somewhere in the cranial archives -- maybe even emerging as a message on that machine that blips away at your vital stats while you're on an operating table -- so listen up:

Daughter is in college and having lots of difficulty with studies and young lads and conflicted ideas about career and marriage and whatever. Father finds daughter ensconced in easy chair watching TV and snacking on leftover chicken to smooth over personal problems and avoid going back to the books for another hack at the homework assignment. What is father's most appropriate action upon seeing his flesh and blood probably adding more flesh and subtracting from candidacy as a beauty queen?

Take a lot of time with your answer.

(A) Ask daughter why she is eating leftovers, since she couldn't possibly be hungry;

(B) Offer to help her with her homework;

(C) Offer to get her to talk about what is troubling her;

(D) Ask daughter if she'd like to meet the scion of a well-heeled family and wouldn't she like to look as attractive as possible before the meeting;

(E) Feel anger welling up inside because the kid is going to screw up everything, so might as well go take a drink or have a smoke until calmer nerves prevail;

(F) Beat the crap out of her because you've told her again and again to watch her weight and this time you're going to teach her a lesson like your family used to teach you; or

(G) Ignore the whole situation and go on with the card game plans for the evening.

There is a trick in this little quiz -- the answer depends on the time frame one is in. In the twenty-first century, the father of the aforesaid noshing daughter has to worry about lawyers and tuition that costs more than the roof over his head. In the nineties, dad thinks about whether his daughter might be good for some financial support in his old age. In the eighties, with all the economic problems and inflation, father was too worried about his own livelihood to get into his daughter's life. Beginning about the seventies, and still true today, the man was lucky if his first wife didn't have the girl in the first place. In the sixties, Father Knew Best. So it shouldn't be too surprising that in the fifties, the belt was mightier than the shrink.

Just because my father chose activity (F) doesn't mean he didn't mean well. Girls were not supposed to be overweight at age seventeen -- he was supposed to put fear into her young heart about what was important. It's not so illogical. Fear has been behind most of human invention for all of written history -- how do you think the Pyramids really got built? Any father that didn't try to whip his daughter into shape had no business even pretending he was the man of the house. THIS IS THE WAY THINGS WERE DONE WHEN HE WAS A KID. So what about the college education and studying problems? Who can remember all of the details? All I can say about it right now is that I didn't get to finish that leftover chicken.

Why do I sometimes get a bright idea which I want to impart to anybody who is within hearing range, even my husband if available, and have to begin the sentence with the word, "Listen." For example, I will say, "Listen, I've just had a great idea about how to solve problem X. . ." Why did I need to start the sentence that way? Am I afraid that I have to announce myself? Have I come to the conclusion that simply opening up my mouth and taking a breath won't get anyone's attention? Listen, is anybody out there? That's just an aside. I tend to get distracted a lot.

I was an emotional eater in those days, and who wasn't? Some girls ate too much, some girls didn't eat enough and some girls had so-called "normal" eating habits. Which reminds me of my most favorite tee-shirt that my daughter bought me just for fun some years ago: The front of the shirt was a cartoon of an empty theatre with one person in the audience. The message on the shirt was: "Convention of adult children of normal parents." When I talk about "normal," I really mean rare and unusual. By simple deductive reasoning, I have come to the conclusion that anything goes, so long as you eat your vegetables. Also, there is nothing wrong with trying to find yourself, if you suspect you might be missing, even if it takes up most of your life.

So when I try to resume the career which somehow got interrupted by fifty-plus years, is it such a big deal? So what if I still have to make sure somebody is paying attention? So what if I have to depend on my Social Security checks while I'm fudging around trying to come out with my giant breakthrough? When I start to worry about what people will think of me for thinking so far outside the box that the box has been thrown in the dumpster a long time ago, I just shrug my shoulders and think about Copernicus. It's good to have heroes that have endured tough odds in a previous millennium. I think about whether he had to start a sentence with the word "Listen," when he announced to people that the Earth was not the center of the universe. He must have had some misgivings too. Didn't he have to get the hell out of town to avoid being punished for being in the wrong place at the wrong time? I have no regrets about the slight delay in my plans. I might not have a brain like Copernicus, but look at the good news -- I hung around and had a pretty good time enjoying the technology that braver and smarter people have given the likes of me. Maybe I was lazy after all, although I've always thought that I really was a lover of hard work. I could sit and watch people doing it all day long. I especially love reading about it, while I'm resting in a comfy chair.

Even after my giant insights hit me in the forehead, I still continued to find myself getting into a vicious cycle of getting distracted from getting distracted. Are you following this? I'm having trouble with it myself. If I were truly lazy and wanted to overeat my way through the rest of my life, then why didn't I do it? I guess I chose the middle fork in the road of gluttony -- I went back to the spinach solution. If you really hate spinach, and you know it is good for you, then what do you do? You mix it with the mashed potatoes. Therefore, if you really hate hard work, but you know it will produce results, then you try to mix up the hard work with something that is fun while you're doing the hard work.

Incredible as it sounds, I used this system to hold onto a job, get back in school, get out of an unfulfilling marriage, raise three kids, have enough money to pay the bills, graduate with a useful degree, do the promotion bit, start a business, keep just enough weight off to avoid the large size department, and have a few laughs along the way. While all this mashed potato-style productivity was going on, feminism took off and I didn't feel so much like an outsider any longer. "Oh, wow," I thought to myself, "now I don't have to prove anything any more!" But I also learned that no matter how hard women want to be treated like men, it just can't be done. The wiring on men and women is as different as AC is like DC. You don't want to find yourself putting the wrong end in the wrong plug.

Every business woman knows what I'm talking about. I just don't have all that testosterone to make people think I'm a cross between a champion fly-weight and a boxing gym-going hunk. I'm much too conditioned by my upbringing and my wiring to punch somebody in the nose if I take offense at how I'm being treated. But I have something men don't have. Don't snicker. I have wiles. I brushed off the dust from an old bag of tricks I used to employ when things got tough -- I learned an effective way to use sarcasm and even a spot of humor to defuse lots of dicey situations. It works most of the time.

The next problem I had to solve is how to avoid running for a tasty treat whenever that inevitable low mood started creeping in. That was a real humdinger of a dilemma! I fudged the solution. I didn't solve the problem. I wound up alternating periods of giving in to periods of hanging tough. On weekdays I eat in such a sensible way, even Oprah Winfrey's cook would admire my resolve. On the weekends I eat more like a greaseball, but like a good little girl, I don't go all the way -- I cheat just enough to stay away from the small sizes department. Maybe that's OK. You have a problem with that?

To summarize this Truth-in-Eating discourse from a veteran up and down, flip-floppy veteran of Weight Watchers and all the rest of those know-it-all diet gurus, I prefer the Rhett Butler© attitude -- I don't really give a damn. (Except I really do -- I'm lying through my artificially whitened teeth!)

WEEKDAYS

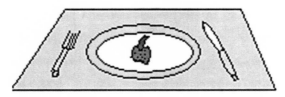

WEEKENDS

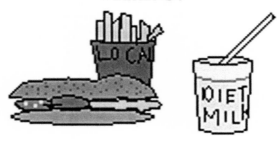

MISS TOOTHPICK'S LUNCH[1]

LO CALORIE KIWI FRUIT

MY LUNCH

---

[1] They didn't have kiwi fruit when I was in high school, but I know that Miss Toothpick would choose that today, if possible.

So in further conclusion, we should tell those brainwashed pediatricians to take refresher courses in childhood eating psychology. Also, they should tell all the mothers of babies with teeth to stock their kitchens with kiwi fruits and tortillas. Oh, and let me add that candy should only be used for picnics so the ants can have fun too. Let the pesky insects have the dental problems.

CHAPTER FOUR
THE GRITTY TRUTH ABOUT
MY SHOPPING

(Not recommended for those in treatment without a note from your doctor)

I learned how to shop before I learned how to talk. How do I know that? I remember that my infant crib was located in my parents'

bedroom, right next to their bed. All my parents talked about, night or day, was my mother's shopping problems. I listened to everything. After I started spouting the usual baby words, mama, dada, me, out, walk, etc., I began to pronounce the words, "return", "pay", "gift", "price", "need", and especially the term, "gotta have."

My toddler wardrobe was in a little makeshift chest in the dining room, because the bedroom was too crowded. In those days, dining rooms were large because people used to have lots of kids and families ate together. My parents were different. They had me and then mysteriously stopped procreating. I don't know if I believed all the excuses as to why my fertile mother didn't quickly conceive again. I secretly harbored the idea that my father feared the cost of everything that a mother could buy for a child while his mind was elsewhere, such as on making a living. Then there was the problem of obsolescence: old dilapidated diapers had to be replaced with stylish new diapers; old rattles lost their charm and were turned in for new ones. Instead of a clickety-clickety sound, they were upgraded to a clickety-clackety one.

The biggest expense turned out to be related to the chubby baby effect: The more food that was stuffed down my darling little mouth, the more I grew into an infant clothes horse. Even in those bygone days when I was a tyke, it was easier to buy new than repair old. The obligatory sewing machine in the dining room not only gathered dust -- it took up valuable space which could better be used with more toy chests and holding areas for kiddies' stuff. The art of sewing was soon replaced by my mom with the art of "a stitch here and a stitch there." This turned out to be nothing more than the needle and thread maneuver as applied to lost buttons and the repair of ripped seams. Bobbins were relegated to fairy tales and were out and quickie mending kits were in.

Before you could utter the words "human growth hormone," which, of course, hadn't been invented yet, but which occurred naturally to an expert eater like me, I outgrew my baby outfits and mom bought me new ones. I promptly ruined these by starting to crawl, then walk and fall, then run and fall, and eventually, while on trips to the park, climb trees -- and fall even further.

Mother worried about how much I used to climb trees -- not so much because my falling caused many boo-boos, but because, even with her quickie mending kits, sewing my slacks back together was difficult and took so much out of her. Mother was one of the original efficiency experts of the household-running routine. It took less time to leg it to the local juvenile shop than it took to put two patches on worn-out knee parts in a pair of corduroy slacks. I added a new word to my vocabulary -- "tsoores." That's what my mother used to call it when she resorted to spending so much of our family budget on new stuff to replace ruined stuff. Poor mother. She hated it when I would beg her to go to the park in Logan Square because she knew what was going to happen there -- yes -- the tree climbing craze would befall me. There was nowhere else for mothers to go to escape the crowded streets in an overdeveloped neighborhood, so she had little choice. The park didn't cooperate either. They had planted low growth climbable trees just for little kids to mess with. It was all a plot to foster consumerism. More trees, more climbing kids, more slacks to buy.

Most of the climbers were little boys because mothers never let their delicate daughters engage in such activities. My mother was no different, but something used to come over me when we went to that tree-filled park -- I thought I was a boy. That's what happens when your parents are trained to avoid sex talk. So I slipped away from mom and took advantage of all those male hormones that slipped through the system and invaded my DNA.

The small chest in the dining room didn't have space enough for new duds and playthings. Mother did her best, however. She kept giving away outgrown wearables and banged up toys to the cleaning lady. I don't think she realized that the cleaning lady's kids might not like mom's taste in children's items, but politeness ruled, and the stuff left our family and went elsewhere. I don't remember feeling bad about the missing outfits. I did feel bad about the Snoopy Sniffer® that wasn't there any longer. I wailed and wailed until mom decided to buy me another one. By the time she actually brought one home, I had outgrown pull toys and had become interested in expensive picture books.

This is the age of euphemisms and verbal correctness. You wouldn't refer to me as a "spoiled brat" any longer. You could refer to me as a "highly indulged youngster," but even the word "indulged" carries a not-so-great connotation. How about calling me a "child of exceptional persuasive abilities?" I could live with that.

Mom and I shopped mostly at Marshall Field's downtown store. Neighborhood stores just didn't have enough of a selection. Kids' clothes were on the Fourth Floor. Unlike the park in Logan Square, the showy Marshall Field store on State Street did cooperate. They filled their entire Fourth Floor with super-appealing kids' toys and clothes for addictive mothers' kids to ogle. They called it the "Glorious Fourth." They could have called it the "Open Your Wallet Fourth," or the "Husbands Beware Fourth, or even the "Wives Sally Forth Fourth." I called it Heaven. Salesladies abounded everywhere. Things were different then when you didn't have to order a search team to find someone to assist you with purchases. They not only took your money with a smile, they gave you gift boxes and, if you really broke your bank with a large purchase, a piece of mint candy for the kid. At Marshall Field, a lollypop was just too plebian. Talk about the seeds of addiction!

When I was a toddler the economy was based on profit and nobody borrowed money. One notable exception to this rule was my father, who never met a banker he didn't try to take to lunch. Daddy lived on borrowed money (and borrowed time also) most of his life, and should have won a prize for the community's highest living off the hog without ever once owning the hog. I did get the impression that most people my folks knew operated in cash only. Income tax wasn't such a big deal then.

These were the War years. Savings Bonds were the thing. I think the Government got by when I was a kid by printing lots of artistic posters, which had a guy in a tall hat pointing his finger at you. Somehow, it seems that most of the cash that didn't fit in peoples' metal boxes (which you couldn't buy any longer because all the metal was melted and recycled into tanks) found its way to the Army and Navy. During that War (when I speak of the War, I mean WWII, not my folks' marriage), we also couldn't buy metal toys any longer, so I had to keep my child-worn seriously dented metal-plated fire truck longer than necessary. I don't know why I was lucky enough to possess a fire truck -- it was supposed to be a boy's toy. I probably told my mother that each of the other boys had one. Maybe mother was duped into buying it for me by an overly aggressive saleslady from Marshall Field who might have suggested it was patriotic. People in those days would do anything to be patriotic. Everything was made to look like an American flag, but you had to be careful about using flaglike clothing for a little kid -- you weren't supposed to pee in it. People were so patriotic and against the enemy that it's a wonder that Mom was able to keep her oriental rug.

I loved my dented toy metal fire truck. I also had a three-foot tall doll buggy made of metal. It was painted the color of Army khaki, but I don't know why. I kept this doll buggy to wheel around my favorite toys and my little bisque charges just like a little mother. One day this buggy and the fire truck mysteriously disappeared. I didn't have anything to say about its disposition. I must have cried a lot when it happened, but my patriotic mother always seemed to smooth over my upset with new accessories for my dolls.

Then there was the rubber stuff. This was readily available until the war effort sucked it all up, except for maybe parts for administering enemas. I had a rubber ball the size of a 12-inch softball with red, white and blue stars and stripes on it. Since I had no playmates to speak of, I mostly threw it against the tree trunks in the park. The squirrels played that game with me -- they had to dart out of the way quickly, because I had such lousy aim. Rubber toys for bathtubs must have been the rage. I commanded a floating menagerie. Yes, the mother ducky was there with its little baby duckies, but I also had a rubber piggy, a rubber chickie and a rubber birdie. This rubber collection was a key component of Mother's system for distracting me while she labored to scrub all the tree bark out of my hair. I hated having my hair soaped because, despite the advertised gentleness, suds still got in my eyes. I used to scream like hell, so mother threatened to put a bar of soap on my tongue if I didn't shut up.

We need another correct term here, because I would never characterize the old school of child discipline as "child abuse." Let's just say that my mother was a pioneer of the art of "child anger management" before it really became famous. But let's also disclose the real deal: the anger management was for her -- not me -- because sometimes she felt like killing me. I never managed my anger at all -- I just kept turning up the volume on my screaming. Where do little kids learn screaming from anyway? Think about it a few moments before you answer. Is there a gene somewhere that says that Family X has a propensity for louder communications than Family Y? It must be so. Nothing else could explain the degree of shrillness and intensity that was common in our household. I am being kind. We were lucky they didn't have noise ordinances back then.

But let's get back to the toys of my kidhood, before I get so emotionally involved here that I have to call a time-out, like they do at a hockey game. I will now launch into a description of the best of the little monster paraphernalia -- the Radio Flyer® pull wagon. Mine was exactly like the ones that they feature nowadays in movies of old tyme coming-of-age films. It was made of metal, all in corroded red with white lettering and a black handle. I put all my stuff in it that wasn't in my metal doll buggy and pulled or pushed. I had one favorite baby doll and I called her Baby Sue. Maybe the store gave her that name. Or maybe some doll designer, I don't know. It had nothing to do with litigation, even though today a parent might engage in that activity if he or she thought the doll might be toxic or bewitched. But I was a good consumer and took better care of that doll than I took care of myself. The doll got her face washed before I washed my own face. That made sense to me, since I could see the doll's face was dirty and I couldn't see my own face because the stupid mirror in our apartment was adult height. At least, that was my argument.

I must have had something to say about what clothes I wanted, because I had a big mouth and hollered when I didn't get my way. But then came the great shoe problem. I liked patent leather black shoes with straps which you wore with white socks with lace cuffs, but my mother found out that I had clubby feet and needed special support. She said I was walking bow-legged. My toes on my right foot were looking at the toes on my left foot. I didn't care if my toes were that friendly, but my mother raised a fit. So she took me to the orthopedic shoe store and bought the ugliest, least fashionable pair of clodhoppers they had in that miserable store. They were Army brown. What good was it to have patriotic-colored shoes when I wasn't allowed to be in the Army? Discovering that I possessed the wrong anatomy for the Army really stamped the fact of girlhood on me. I knew early on that they weren't going to take me and I've never forgiven God about that. Yes, I knew about the WACS and the WAVES, but that seemed like sissy stuff to me. They wore skirts. Guys wore the real gear.

This early-in-life disappointment for me was the beginning of my future shopping addiction. It was reverse psychology operating in a subtle manner. If I didn't get to choose my own shoes when I was little, then, oh boy, wait until I grew up, would I show those grown-ups! All my own money, as soon as I earned it, was going to go on shoes and clothes of my choosing and big person's toys and everything! You can see for yourself how the momentum built up for my future spendthrift ways. I began laying plans while still a peanut.

In my box of memorabilia, I still have a photo taken of me when I was about four years old with my tin buggy and a horn, the rubber ball and my dolly sticking out of it. The photographer probably didn't realize it, but whoever it was had captured my pouting face. There it was, for the entire world to see -- the beginning of my discontent. I have the proof in an old wrinkled silver gelatin print. I was probably pouting because I didn't want to be photographed wearing a silly old jumper and blouse. My dolly had a newer outfit than I did. Life was so unfair that I made a decision to outsmart everybody from then on so that I could have everything I wanted. Ha Ha! I not only had a lot to learn -- I acquired a book about how to do it! Little Orphan Annie© had been published as a child reader. All I had to do was find my own Daddy Warbucks©. Well, I'm getting ahead of myself here.

As disappointing as life was for me, with so many postponed pleasures, things got much worse when I approached puberty. I had noticed that all the other girls owned many form-fitting sweaters. Most were cashmere. For those of you who live in the very warm South and have never seen snow or experienced frostbite, cashmere is an expensive wool which is very soft. The important point about cashmere sweaters during my getting-to-puberty years is that all the girls who cared about them counted how many each girl had. One girl had 25 of them. That gave her the upper hand. Her name was Barbara. I was jealous of her for a lot of reasons besides her sweater inventory, and I have a bias about females with the name, Barbara. Can't help it, folks, early influences never die. I wanted to do damage to Barbara's good name by spreading the rumor that her folks had to do without proper food in order to fund Barbara's sweater passions. What else could explain why a twelve-year-old girl owned so many expensive sweaters? And to fuel my upset even more, she looked so good in them! She had red hair too. That made the whole thing even worse. I have a bias about females with red hair. Of course, my own reddish hair today comes out of a bottle, and I would not dream of letting my gray roots get too obvious.

My mother was not talented at consulting with other mothers about appropriate dress for a daughter, because she kept buying me white blouses and cardigan sweaters which were not only not cashmere, but they were rather rough on my delicate skin. She dressed me like a bookworm. Well, I was a bookworm, but she didn't have to advertise it to everybody! If a girl like me didn't wear a pullover sweater but instead wore a plain blouse with a nondescript cardigan, she got her nose punched in and her hair yanked out. You see, what I didn't realize in seventh grade was that girls who could spell and do math reasonably well wore a special type of outfit which broadcast the fact that she was studious. Now I wasn't really studious -- I simply had this history of reading books by myself because I had no social life. But somehow what I wore and how I acted was enough reason for better-dressed girls to fail to invite me to the best birthday parties. I did win a small battle and finally became the owner of about ten cashmere pullover sweaters, but we paid a heavy price for that indulgence. My mother had to lie to my dad about how much she paid for them and I had to camouflage them with very large scarves whenever I wore them. It was the kind of deception of which marital rifts are made.

My mother should have stood up to me and maybe beat the crap out of me if I hollered about always needing stylish clothing. But these were the booming years right after the war and parents had to make up for their own lack of joyful possessions during the Great Depression. They indulged their own fancies on their kids and I was an indulgee. In our social circles people were judged by appearances and my mother was caught up in the great wave of luxury spending which contributed to the Post-War boom. Dads kept working like mules to provide while housewives made out lengthy shopping lists. Nevertheless, he was a co-conspirator. He loved to give mother surprises. She had admired a certain mink coat in the local furrier's window, so my dad became famous in the neighborhood for bringing it home to her in a grocery store paper shopping bag. This purchase, plus others I can't enumerate, probably helped to eliminate my future college fund. I can't believe I am controlling myself while I write this down -- I am going to take a break now by thumbing through the latest issue of the hottest fashion magazine in my pile of reading material.

Ah, that felt good.

Somewhere along the line I determined that it was probably a good idea to become rich. Rich kids seemed to suffer less. I am now thinking back to an episode I experienced as a third grader, where three rich girls tried to beat up on me. We had recently moved to this neighborhood which consisted of homes above our means. I believe we were the only renters on the block. Also, we didn't fit in. We had the wrong religion and didn't vote for the right guy for President, and a bunch of other stuff, but I don't want to get too melodramatic and miss my point here. Well, I fought back against those three girls and damaged the hairdos and outfits of all three. I had learned to use my fists by watching boys play rough and sitting through a lot of old Western movies. While the girls were trying to protect their lovely dresses, using female tactics, I had no such inhibitions. I drew blood and gave them each a lesson in ambushed tomboy violence. Although I went home all disheveled and crying, a referee would have awarded me some hellova prize for underdog excellence in delivering three technical knockouts. No girl messed with me after that, rich, poor or middle class.

A new skill became part of my repertoire that year -- the stifling of tears. I had to practice a lot and tried it while slicing onions, but that didn't work very well. For awhile I dreamed that some day I might do well as a female boxer, but in reality I couldn't stand pain. I did love the thrill of winning, however, even if it was just an argument. Not long after that fighting incident, my folks felt very guilty and moved out of that neighborhood, but they lost lots of heated debates with me from then on. I had gained priceless leverage by holding my ground during that surprise three-girl guerilla attack. I used my newly gained power to acquire a fresh library of Judy Bolton© mystery books. The pace of my reading went from about two books per week to at least four. And I demanded that none of my precious books ever be disposed of without my consent. Naturally, I had no intention of ever giving any such consent.

One of the many turning points in my brief existence on the planet had occurred. I made up my mind how I was going to deal with the dilemmas in life. It was similar to going solo without flying lessons. Now I had graduated from being a child of exceptional persuasive abilities to an adolescent possessed of staunch principles. In other words, when it came to getting my way, I was the most stubborn cuss around. Nobody could change my mind about anything! Oh my, I almost hate myself for having to relive these emotional hurts which probably contributed to my future shopping addiction. But not enough to go through my clothes closets and weed out the things I never wear.

I had lots of dreams about all different careers I might have. Who would have thought back then that when I reached my mid-life crisis, I would make it my business to shop a lot and have an endless supply of easy money? But my plans were flawed. Although my mother kept trying to drill into me the necessity of marrying a good provider, I just didn't get it. I thought I was going to earn a great deal of money myself some day. Why didn't I have the foresight to invent plastic credit cards? Yes, I know plastic didn't get really popular until that movie, "The Graduate©" was a hit. But I had to have come in contact with *something* plastic! I already had the borrowing part down pat. I have searched my memory over and over, but the nearest thing resembling plastic which I can remember from my childhood was *elastic*! My underpants stayed up most of the time, didn't they? Somewhere in my brain is the first glimmering of the way to live on credit without owing your life to bankers. Mr. Hill had already published the book "Think and Grow

Rich©," but my thoughts ran along the lines of a hypothetical title I could have authored -- "Live Rich and Skip the Thinking."

I may have gotten one idea of how to get stuff without having to worry about running up bills I couldn't pay -- I only needed to buy stuff -- I didn't need to keep it! I got this idea from my mother. Who had room in the house anyway for all the stuff out there? I could buy items I wanted for cash, get to look at all those items, even keep the gift boxes, and then return the stuff to get the cash to buy more stuff! Then, I could go out all over again and recycle the whole thrill of it. There is little doubt in my mind that these thoughts were the origin of a new type of thrill I would enjoy in my later life -- the collector's craze. That craze was made for the likes of me. My future phase of lunacy was just beginning to gel.

I wish I could blame my spendthrift problems on other people. That's a syndrome which has flourished recently, as the age of being a needy victim is now an important part of our popular culture. Looking back on my own situation, I can't truly pretend that I didn't know what I was getting into. Today it is almost fashionable for folks to overspend and overuse credit, but I came from a special hotbed of post-war entrepreneurial activity. My dad, at his most successful, saw cash streaming in like nothing he had ever known and must have thought it would go on forever. In my household, financial decisions were made by who screamed most vehemently and who gave in first. I extracted something quite positive from the experience. Today, I could easily teach a course on what not to do both in marriage and in budgeting with the goal that some young souls pick up on it. I wish I had taken photos of some of the arguments in process, because they would have made a great slide show. What I can do is include at the end of this chapter a picture of my now obsolete credit cards, because one picture of too many credit cards might be worth thousands in visual head-thumping amazement.

The next part of this saga of my spending mania is the part where **any** psychologist reading this will probably foam at the mouth and go into an analytic high.

I can officially trace the origins of my descent into financial chaos to certain turning points which involve both my deceased father and my deceased cousin, Lee. Neither of them is likely to judge me harshly. It's more likely that I acquired certain weaknesses by emulating my mother's behavior, but I've done enough bashing of that poor woman, who ought to be able to rest her weary soul in eternal peace. My nearly drowning in a pit of red ink as an adult started with some escapism into the world of sports as a kid.

It was my father that got me into the Love of the Game of Baseball. Daddy took me to the Cubs games as often as he could, not because he was trying to entertain his darling daughter, but because he got stuck caring for me whenever my mother had to give the house a thorough cleaning with me out of the way. Besides, like most North Side Chicagoans with any sense of baseball knowledge, going to the Cubs games was better than having religion -- you prayed when they lost and you prayed when they won that they wouldn't lose the next game on the schedule. Now everybody who follows sports knows that the Cubs won the pennant in the year 1945. They played Detroit and lost that series. I had attended Cubs games before that year with my dad and his buddy, Marcus, but it is unclear to me whether my dad actually attended one of the series games in Chicago. Marcus was enough of a big shot to have gotten tickets, but would they have taken me? Probably not. Still, I brag to my so-called friends that I attended the 1945 World Series. Now you may ask, what the hell does this have to do with my shopping addiction? Well, I'm getting to that. Be very patient, because I must tell this in my own way, and that way is to grind it out, episode by episode! I picked up that habit from watching numerous serials on TV.

I got interested in sports and in ballplayers because, as a certified tomboy who had leaped from one three-story building to the next three-story building and had owned a metal fire truck, I thought that guys' activities were even more fun than girls' activities. I don't even remember what girls did for fun in 1945, but I guarantee that most of them didn't know or even want to know how to slide into second base on a steal. I actually played the game with young boys on our street corner, and my mother thought it was better for me to have fun playing with the boys than nagging her for even more games and clothes before she had the next money-spending excuse ready. Playing corner baseball actually wasn't better -- but it was cheaper. So Daddy got me interested in baseball as an outlet and soon I was listening to games on the radio and decided I wanted to be a sportscaster when I grew up. This was one of the earlier conceived careers I remembered having as a goal. I thought the life would be exciting, because Bert Wilson, the announcer for the Cubs, used to scream at the top of his lungs every time a Cub player got a hit. A home run meant that the screaming lasted longer. Screaming was right up my alley. I already had the background experience from listening to my folks at their best, but I knew I needed to practice.

Now where could a kid practice baseball announcer type screaming without attracting too much attention? My next door neighbor used to give trumpet lessons, and those loud noises would drown out almost everything. So during those sessions I used to go in our garage behind our house and practice yelling "Here comes the pitch! It's a curve! Oh, he missed it by a foot! Yeah!!!" And then I would catch my breath and start all over again. Eventually, I would get a sore throat. I really wasn't sure about being a sports announcer. How many could they hire? And when? And if the Army would never take me, why did I think that Mr. Wrigley would be any different? I never discussed these concerns with anyone. Nobody listened to me anyway.

One of my weaknesses was the lack of persistence I showed for pursuing personal ambition. Anybody could squash my delicate ego with the wrong remark at the wrong time. For example, when I would do my best to mimic Bert Wilson -- "There goes the ball -- it's really traveling -- is it, can it be, dare we hope, yes, it is, Andy Pafko has just slammed the ball over the center field wall for a home run!!!!!" -- at first I thought I had it just right, including the ear-splitting holler. But then doubt would creep in. My mother would say to me, "It's your bedtime, put on your pajamas." My father would say to me, "You heard your mother!" The boys on the block blocked out my very good imitation of Bert Wilson and said, "Girls don't broadcast sports, Miss Dopey!" The next door neighbor lady, who really adored me, said, "Don't even think of becoming a celebrity, like my husband, you'll have a difficult home life." She was nice to me and her husband really was a celebrity bandleader. She said to me, "You have a real talent for music, and you should try that." My mother said to me, "Practice your piano lessons." My father said to me, "You heard your mother!" The boys on the block said, "You probably stink."

Kids with secure egos don't worry about what others think. Very few kids in those days had secure egos. As I speak, I think about my husband. He definitely was one of the exceptions, and he actually did do for a living what he said he might do, and his parents thought that everything he did was wonderful and God-Given. My parents thought that everything I did was annoying and that I didn't listen. Since my Mom was really ruled by my Dad, the financial provider of the household, I have decided to blame my Dad for getting me interested in sports and then not helping me become Bert Wilson's successor.

Wait a minute, I think you're thinking, what does all this garbage I just made you read have to do with having a shopping addiction? Well, I haven't yet described how my knowledge of sports enticed me many years later to go to a sports card convention where my cousin, Lee, was exhibiting his wares. I was like a drunk making a visit to a liquor warehouse. There, at the convention, were all the old baseball cards and other sports collectibles that had slipped through the cracks when everyone's mothers were throwing that stuff in the trash during cleaning fits. The items being peddled, some bought at black market and others brought out of carefully storaged cubbyholes, were now on display by kids who weren't even alive yet when the items were first issued. I was not a typical attendee at this event, not just because I was female, but because I was a middle-aged lady who had actually dodged foul balls in grandstand seats in the forties and fifties when the guys pictured in the cards ran the bases in baggier uniforms. The most impressive booth of all was operated by my cousin, Lee. I stood near him and watched him rake in sweaty dollar bills from kids, some of whom were too small to even reach the top of his display table. What a way to make some pin money! I got much too excited thinking about involving myself in this craze because I still recall that adrenalin rush -- the exhilarating act of panting over a new activity on an otherwise dull weekend. I got sucked into the mania of it all the way a choc-a-holic might get high during a first excursion to Hershey, Pennsylvania. And that, folks, was the beginning of my collecting binge.

There's more dark stuff about my collecting binge than I am ready to admit, because then I won't be the only person, besides my husband, who knows how nuts I got over trying to make a living as a collectibles dealer. Suffice it to say that I spent about five years trying to turn a binge into a business, and I was lucky to get out of it with my credit intact. It was only a sideline, but I needed a life, didn't I? Oh boy, did I go crazy trying to get back at my father? Or was I just desperate to find something interesting in my life? My vote goes to the latter as a reason for my motivation. I got some positives out of this phase, however. I picked up an awful lot of knowledge about sports stars and trading card shows, which might be useful to me some day in a trivia competition.

Blaming others for one's own mistakes is more fun when you don't take this blame too far. I learned that even before I went to a shrink. In fact, I almost didn't need to go to a shrink at all -- I could have been one myself. But that's getting into some other long spiel, and you already know I have no patience at all.

After the card collecting mania, I started going to antique shows and then I got into Barbie® Doll collecting. I had held in my hand, in the year 1959, the very first Barbie Doll ever manufactured -- the one with the black and white striped bathing suit. It had been bought by my first husband's cousin's wife for her ten-year-old daughter. The wife thought it was too adult-looking of a doll for her kid, but she let the kid play with it anyway. She should have left it in the box and put it away, but she didn't have a crystal ball -- she had a doll-loving daughter. Most kids played with their first Barbie dolls, you know, took off the bathing suit, the high heels, etc., and put the doll in the bathtub with them, stuff kids did with dolls.

Years later, when the collecting mania became more broadly publicized, I remembered holding that skinny plastic icon in my hands and kicking myself for not recognizing a gold mine out there. So I bought Barbie dolls later on, but I missed out on making a killing. The smartest thing I ever did as a collector was to buy Michael Jordan 1989 Fleer® rookie cards, which I later sold for a big profit, but all that did was to nearly make me whole again. Just think: if I had pursued my very first instinct and become a baseball announcer, I could have been a legend today. Instead, I'm just your basic weirdo story-teller, reviewing dreams of the wealth and fame that got away. I even sold my Exxon stock about twenty years too soon. To quote Holly GoLightly©, "Golly Gee!" (Whew, nobody really uses that expression any longer.)

After I emerged from the bumps and bruises of my childhood and grew up into a productive adult (which some people who know me dispute). I began to earn a serious living at the practice of law. I was single at the time. That's when I carried the collecting craze to a new extreme -- buying expensive art. I bought paintings, sculptures, antiques and a new town house in the suburbs to showcase my newly acquired objects. I was slowly morphing into an updated version of my shopping bag-toting father and my appearance-obsessed mother, but something in my heredity must have subjected me to a disease of a more virulent strain. I was a consumer with a death wish. There have been case studies made of my type of spending, but I did it with more of a flourish. It is well known that wealthy people buy genuine art to adorn their numerous residences and eventually to supply museums and support curators and their ilk. It's a good thing and helps keep a number of accomplished artists in higher tax brackets. However, no matter how you slice the loaves of bread that I earned, or judge the right and wrong of a single woman's spending choices, there can be only one conclusion as to my diagnosis arrived at by normal people -- complete nut job, out of control and headed for financial turmoil. I was just a simple working girl. Maybe I should leave out the word "simple." I was a complex of complexes, a product of a shaky set of values, and a train on the wrong track. When monthly Master Card and Visa bills which arrived in my mailbox totaled more than my annual take home pay, I took immediate action -- I had my credit lines increased. Gallery owners were probably onto me, but they never had qualms about transferring my debt obligations for purchases to the big credit card giants. I can truthfully say that I never did buy an item of art which I could afford.

Now that all this is out on the table (or on the walls or in the curio cabinet), I can get to the truth under the truth: I finally stopped buying and reversed course before a single credit card bill was paid late. I did this by dunking my head into a figurative bucket of ice water -- I got married to a frugal play-by-the-rules shopping avoider. Not every over- spender can use this system successfully. But it can work well for a person conscious of her self image going into a third marriage. My new husband not only hates shopping for clothing and non-essentials -- he remains at least one hundred feet from the entrance of any store I go into. Think of the rules for placement of a "Vote For Joe Blow" election sign near a polling place, and you can get the idea of how my husband operates and where you can find him when I'm in a store. In spite of my stated disclaimer, I really do advocate this as a remedy for any self-respecting shop-a-holic who wants to go for the cure and deal with the withdrawal pains of visiting art galleries and leaving with only the free brochures. I recommend that credit card abusers and stuffomaniacs consider this type of approach to mend their evil ways and coax bankruptcy lawyers into another line of work. Buying stuff is only a different form of acquiring love, and you might as well have the real thing.

I do not believe that credit cards should be shredded or that a recovering buying freak has to go in the opposite direction and become a have-nothing junkie either. You do not have to live like my younger son, who can easily put his complete set of worldly possessions into the trunk of his car. Just do the following: Take a deep breath and say to yourself: "I will not keep the American economy rolling all by myself -- I will reach out to others and, with a straight face and an iron will, tell all the upwardly mobile Jones families they can go screw themselves." (Note: You don't have to actually tell these people that out loud -- you can write it down somewhere and hide it under the piles on your desk.)

Since this brief review of my personal nonsense is supposed to be about the truth, I have a confession: Instead of a shop-a-holic today, I am a computer gamer-a-holic, a piles-of- crap-on-my-desk-a-holic and a virtue-a-holic. That last one is the subject of another expose another time.

I really didn't intend for this chapter to end with a message of utter thrift and addiction conversion syndrome, but it happened anyway. Nobody's perfect.

CHAPTER FIVE
THE TRUTH ABOUT MY
FEMININITY
(Identity issues and other tirades)

First of all, why in the world are you reading a chapter about such a non-earth-shaking item as my femininity when there are so many more grave matters in the world that should concern you? Or are you, as I am, trying to avoid thinking too deeply about said grave matters too often? It's the same thing that older people encounter when they realize that they are getting closer and closer to eternity -- who really wants to dwell on that eventuality a lot of the time? Isn't levity supposed to be a cure for scowl lines? If we can't have levity some of the time, then we will all end up looking like those German soldiers did at the end of the film, "Raiders of the Lost Ark."©

I need a very light touch when it comes to my secrets of survival as a woman. Lots of folks have hinted to me that I often display characteristics that could be interpreted as, uh, well, sort of male. Let me be perfectly clear about this: I don't often wear what I consider an anachronistic item known as a dress -- not because I'm opposed to ladies' clothes, but because I find slacks and jeans more comfortable. Well, there's another angle to this -- with a dress, a woman has to decide if she will wear hose, go bare-legged or wear anklets. I have a very dear friend who wears anklets (otherwise known as socks), but she also wears very long skirts and is quite tall. She looks just fine to me, but I would always be afraid that if I wore a very long skirt, it would get caught in my bicycle spokes, or something even more ominous. An astute reader, such as yourself, might point out, and rightly so, that I could always change into shorts for bicycle riding. Well, that's just ducky! It sounds very much like good logic and sensible advice. Who do you think you are, my husband? This is me -- the stubborn cuss! You see, I have to factor in my constant need to save time and effort. The truth is, I have enough problems with my closet and dresser drawers as it is. Oh, let's just stow it! I can't get into all my problems now because I am not authoring an encyclopedia on my schtick.

I do wear dresses occasionally, but I definitely restrict that wearing to formal occasions, such as weddings of people who have an audience, and, maybe, oh yes, if I have to go to court to fight a ticket for loitering near the men's washroom, or some such nonsense. And while it's completely untrue that I purchase and even wear jockey shorts, I have been observed in clothing stores looking at piles of new jockey shorts. Sometimes I even touch the jockey shorts, just to be sure that they are really made of whatever they're supposed to be made of. Don't get any of the wrong ideas here -- I touch all kinds of stuff.

If someone really tries to question my feminine side, I think about some defensible reason why I am like I am, but I prefer to change the subject to something else. My favorite alternative topic is the sticky Florida weather in July.

Nevertheless, I think I should set the record straight as to my femininity. But before I launch into a new tiresome tirade about this issue, I need to set forth a few definitions:

FEMININITY - A cumbersome word, difficult at best to pronounce, even more difficult to define, which I believe has to do with loving lace curtains and getting a thrill out of washing one's mate's wearables, perhaps even going so far as to iron them. When women have this characteristic, they usually have many frilly things in closets and drawers and pack them in luggage when they go to the out-of-town Spa. The degree to which a person has this characteristic depends on how many times the lady (or, in certain cases, her poodle dog or Angora cat) has her nails done in a month.

FEMINISM - A noun. I actually looked this up in the Oxford American College Dictionary©, which I still possess, long after I dropped out of my first college. It says that this word is: "the advocacy of women's rights on the grounds of political, social, and economic equality to men." Wow, I'll bet that one was edited and re-edited before they printed it, and definitely by a committee of extremely equal women! OK, I would add the following to the consensus definition: The quality of being pissed off because you were born a woman, and you're going to really sock it to all the men by legislating their gender into extinction by the year 2090. On the way to that neutering goal, feminism mandates that women outnumber men in every profession except dust maid, which position will be filled by the best and the brightest of the rocket scientists, who will only have been born in test tubes. Einstein's Theory of Relativity will be renamed "Gertrude's Philosophy of Universal Truth." I think that ought to do it for the time being.

FEMALE - or, as in forms to be filled out, "F." This is an easy one. There are only two possibilities -- female or male. If you're an "F" then you know what kind of underwear you will be forced to wear for the rest of your life, at least in proper company. However, in the unlikely instance that you don't know whether you're an "F" or an "M", I suggest you bring some identification with you -- better have it at all times.

FEMINIZE: A word that conservative talk show hosts use at least once a week, but only on the weeks where they're not off somewhere playing golf. I think it means that new populist desire to give sissy names to everything you ever heard of, including toilet paper, which will most likely be renamed "derrière cleansing fabric." The trucks which transport this product and other similar items will be renamed "motor shehicles" and the personnel womanning them will be renamed "truckists." Dictionaries will soon be multi-volumed because almost all descriptive words will be two and three words, where one used to suffice.

I wish I didn't have to include anything at all about how a woman takes care of her nails, but this is another problem for me. I have nails that break constantly. I know I'm not the only one this happens to, but why are my nails so brittle? In the last fifteen years or so we have all seen a proliferation of nail salons and artificial nail kits. I tried artificial nails once for one of the few weddings I got invited to recently, and I couldn't be my normal self. Everything I had to do revolved around my nails -- whether it was shaking someone's hand or grabbing my purse or knocking on the rest room door -- I had to keep guarding my fingers and checking on the gluing job. I used to have excuses for sporting nasty nails, such as gardening or extensive craft projects, or lifting sacks of potatoes, etc., but I don't even do those things any more. So why do I still resist having frequent manicures like other ladies do? Well, it's because I'm a klutz. Once a klutz, always a klutz. Now I think I'm too old to acquire new nail care habits. I quiver and quake when I realize that I shouldn't be constantly cleaning out the crud under my fingernails with my Swiss army knife. You see, there is something about my early rebellion against my mother's teaching that has stayed with me. Do I have to expose all my unresolved issues in only one little book? Leave me alone about my nails and my dislike of wearing dresses.

OK, I think you understand how I feel about my femininity, just from scanning my definitions. I have a different problem, however. I have no clue as to whether I've been the victim of sexism because for years I have walked around thinking that everyone else was normal and I was the one who had the loose connection somewhere in the neurosphere. I know what most guys think of my driving because I can read lips and fingers pretty well. I refer to everybody as "sir" when I think I am being addressed, and then I turn around to see what sex the person is. I give young hunky waiters with dangling earrings the benefit of the doubt and probably over tip. I make "koochee koochee koo" to babies in shopping carts being wheeled by long-haired sweaty gorillas wearing wife-beater undershirts. I take a number at a delicatessen take-out counter even when there's no one else in line if I think the bagel handler looks like a family man with a bad attitude. I'm very conscious of having lived through several years' worth of long queues at the entrances to women's bathrooms and I respect the construction types who made the toilet bases crooked because the job was underbid. I'm timid at pari-mutuel windows staffed by men smoking cigars, especially when I have a winning ticket, and I go out of my way to avoid the path of a policeman pursuing a little old grandmother fruit stand thief.

I was raised to respect the fact that I wasn't promised in marriage at age fourteen and didn't have to have my feet bound or take a nap while the men folk were discussing politics. I was lucky to have lived through the fifties without having to buy a single pair of platformed high heels. I have come to terms with the sex that I am because it's a wonderful sex. I'm not joking about a lot of these important little details, no matter how trivial, because I really like being a woman. Think of all the fun I had bearing my three children -- everyone I knew felt sorry for me and brought flowers. I'm such a short woman that of late I have had to tell certain of my co-workers to cut out the little old lady jokes.

Most men treat me with a great deal of respect. I would like to say that my husband always treats me with a great deal of respect, but since this essay is about being truthful, let's just say that the respect scales tip a little in his favor, especially when we're both sitting on the sofa trying to watch a baseball game.. I don't let it get to me because sarcasm is his defining characteristic. I love the way he pauses for a few minutes to let me catch up with him when we're going from our parked car to the restaurant. I feel apologetic when I speak out of turn, even when I'm talking in my sleep. However, I often fear that I'm not always as respectful around men as I should be. Most men still avoid punching me out when I insult them, simply because they were brought up correctly. I like being the weaker sex. I always ask my husband to lift things which I probably could do myself, except that I resist toning up my muscles, even when the flab under my arms hangs longer and longer each day and I am forced into the use of headbands around my loose arm skin so that I can be distinguished from a reptile.

I have never even once been referred to as a "babe," having been born too early, and also, because of a technical problem which occurred during my gestation, rendering my hips measuring the square of the usual number. I would have liked to look like a babe, even for a month, because I would have liked to know how it felt to be whistled at while at work instead of being asked to bring the files into the conference room after I complete fixing my hair. I'm not resentful, really, not even a little bit, no, not even a tiny atom, not even a quark's worth. God D---- It, I said I'm not resentful! Oh, go (bleep) yourself! Get Out of here!!!!

I love to write extremely ladylike verse. The poet in me rises every morning with a deliciously literary idea. It gels and crystallizes over breakfast and then something strange happens -- mainly while I'm using the restroom. It turns into drivel and dries up like a turd in the sun -- in Phoenix. But I nourish the hope that it will reflower in my mind and show up on the filthy computer screen. I forgot to mention that if my husband doesn't proffer his screen cleaner once in awhile, I probably would have to buy a new computer. Anyway, I will try to resurrect my thought of the morning, today, if possible:

The air is as fresh as a courtesan's whisper
It undulates through the fragile new growth of the versatile pine
Lithely bending before the murmuring westerly breezes
And lingers before my delicate proboscis
In the morn
My husband got out of bed before me
And is making pancakes.

You see, I am really a feminist at heart. I'm probably the worst kind of all. I won't even admit it to myself. But really, people, I just love truckers, and I never want them to change anything about the way they truck, or the way they hang tough, or the way they just, well, hang. I don't even want them to avoid eye contact with me, so long as it's just for a split second. I worry about the future when I might need a cane to walk comfortably because I've been walking like a retired football player for the last thirty years. Do you think I'm not self-conscious about my short-comings? I'll get over feeling self-conscious when I finally learn once and for all which side of the refrigerator contains the onions and where I have stashed all my missing books. I'll laugh things off just like a guy when I pick out a handbag from my closet and there aren't twenty-seven Courtyard by Marriott ballpoint pens inside. I'll get over all the little slights I have suffered most of my life because I never got to see a parade without poking someone in the behind or excusing myself in the midst of a movie without stumbling onto a gentleman's lap. All these little annoyances will disappear as soon as I no longer have to ask someone taller than me what the hell happened when a crowd is gathered around an accident scene. It's really OK to be a short woman because I have picked up way more than my share of nickels and pennies from parking lots. I enjoy being a gal, and maybe it's a good thing that I never got into the Army because who needs a klutz with a gun?

I have to applaud myself for not contaminating this piece of "literature" I have written with one of my many rhyming poems. However, I can't resist sticking one of them in right here and right now -- here goes:

CREATIVITY AND THE SEXES

Are women more creative than men?
I've pondered this again and again
Well, the Muses were chicks

And the Beachboys were hicks
But who cares, this is Now, that was Then
Guys had steam rooms while women gave birth
There were mostly male scribes here on earth
While the men drank all night,
Keeping women out of sight,
They monopolized most written mirth;
But that's only history, it seems
If you really believe in your dreams
With no Y chromosome,
Can you still drive it home?
With desire you, gal, can write reams!
Or if stand-up comedy is your bent
Don't get upstaged and don't be content
If a guy would outdo you,
Just flatly go, "Screw You!"
You can easily outclass the gent.

Why waste time on a sexual war?
Just create while he's deep in a snore
You simply wake earlier
While you make your hair curlier
As he's shaving you even the score;
The big failing which all men have got
Is their arrogance, and they have a lot
While they're gloating all day
You're creating away
And come up with material that's hot!
Most men disdain baths, they take showers
But women bathe creatively for hours

While my man's getting dressed
I'm there fashioning my best
Bathing sharpens my literary powers!
So while hubby works at his computer
Or perhaps he's a fast-track commuter
It doesn't matter which,
You amazing hot bitch,
Your work's finished and without any tutor!
See, the stuff in your multi-tasked head
Worked itself out while you were in bed
You remembered it all
So when editors call,
You've got gems which they've never ever read!

07/11/07

Please, dear Lord, let me go on being a feminine woman for as long as my days here on the cleaned-up planet allow. And while you're at it, Lord, please don't take the rest of my hair away. Or my smoothness of complexion. Or my delicate disposition. And I hate to mention it, but I need a way to get rid of this f-----'g cellulite.

And screw the varicose veins and the dried up you know what and the black holes on my face. And another thing, ...

CHAPTER SIX
THE TRUTH ABOUT MY
INTELLIGENCE

(This one is a bit spacey, so you down-to-earth types can skip it)

I have always respected the intelligence of babies, but I don't think we egomaniac grown-ups have the foggiest perception of how dumb we are compared to babies. I will attempt to relate the foregoing premise to my own situation.

It is my firm belief that I began life with the mentality of a genius, and then they dumbed me down. (I really get it on with that phrase.) They must have dumbed me down steadily and systematically from day One to get me down to their level. Who is "they?" We must start with the hospital personnel. They knew how to respect my medical and physical needs and did their best, but they could not have possibly respected my intellect. I still have that little beaded bracelet that they used to identify infant from infant and match each little brat up with its mother. Now I knew who I was -- I was a kicking, screaming monster just waiting to put the first possible object available in my mouth because one's mouth is the primary learning tool of most primates. I say most, because I know my former dog, Mattie (short for Matilda, because she was a waltzing kind of dog), learned more stuff with her nose than her mouth. Humans are mouth learners.

Just observe the typical infant: It doesn't get confused about its emotions. Things are simple: "I'm hungry, I hurt, I'm wet, I'm bored, I'm stinky, I'm restless, I don't like this position you've got me in and I can't do anything about it until I build up these weak muscles I've gotten saddled with. Etc., etc. So you dumbass human big shot, you, get with the program!"

Babies are so busy learning the jargon coming out of people's mouths they don't have time to speak early. To speak too early would be dumb. Some grown-up people haven't learned that lesson yet. They were really dumbed down. Just watch an idiot grown-up who habitually puts his foot in his mouth with everything he says. Chances are one or both of his parents or child care enthusiasts damaged that poor soul's thinking ability in some way. I have some individuals in mind, but I'm still not quite dumb enough to give names. The reason that some of the brightest babies don't talk right away is that they are the best listeners and are sizing up the situation before saying the wrong thing. They're checking out all the details they need to juggle in order to satisfy their needs and wants. Now what's more intelligent than that? Modern dumbass people don't check out enough details -- that's why dumb crooks get caught and feckless investors lose their hard-earned money in the wrong investments. A new baby wouldn't be so dumb as to invest in a tired stock <u>after</u> it has hit its high and started to go down. It takes years to become that dumb.

I know that I was horribly dumbed down as I grew up, and the process began extremely early. Here's my proof: A baby seems to visualize solutions to things without even reading the instructions or attending lectures. Ever see a one-year-old succeed at putting a round wooden peg into just the right shaped hole? First, the kid tastes the peg -- hmmm, doesn't seem nourishing, but feels good against the swelling gums. Then the kid waves the peg around, which is an excellent exercise for developing arm muscles. Don't you agree that this is an intelligent thing to do? Finally, the kid looks at the wooden board with the different shape holes and tastes the board. Realizes it also isn't food, but it was some kind of challenge. That's good for self-assurance. Soon it starts knocking the round peg all over the place and maybe knocks the wrong thing, like mother's tiled floor, and makes a mark on it. That's good for building up aggression, which will be needed as soon as another small person starts competing with it. Finally, the tyke tries making the connection and realizes that the round peg was supposed to go in the round hole -- not the square one. That's what the grown-up wanted the tyke to do. But what the hell good is that connection? It's not going to get its hunger satisfied nor its diaper changed. OK, when the kid is adult enough to decide if it wants to become an engineer, it's better to put the round peg in the round hole. I don't want to demean Fisher-Price at this point.

Now I'm going to get to my original point, which is how I was dumbed down for so many years, I can't count them. I ask my husband, "Honey, I can't figure out this new remote for the DVD player, can you help me?" After I don't get the satisfaction of being helped, which I should have known in the first place, I finally, after numerous trials and errors, figure it out. Of course, I had to read the instructions five times after discovering where my own spoken language was on the multi-folded tiny scrap of paper that I nearly threw out. After pushing a few buttons around, I'm happy if I haven't permanently programmed something weird into the new remote. Sometimes I discover that all I'm able to play on the DVD is the segment on how the director of the film captured the destruction of the village without killing a bunch of people. I am unable to play the movie itself, of course. Now, how dumb is that?

A baby would have little or no problem with the new remote. It would bite on it and feel good that all the little buttons felt just great against those aching gums, and that mother would soon come to give it real food, which is much more nurturing and useful than any of the crap that shows up on those DVD movies. Babies are much smarter than adults at determining cause and effect and making intelligent choices. Food comes before time-wasting movie watching and little babies just know it!

Now, I am getting to the point of the little drawing at the beginning of this rambling muck I have laid out for you sucker readers. Einstein was considered one of the smartest adults in the world, and even he was dumbed down, but he was able to keep some of the sense in his head even as an older guy. As a little child, he had to be able to grasp concepts of relativity and time, because he was the first one to write some papers on it in the whole world. He also realized early in life that it wasn't going to be easy explaining the stuff to others. They didn't have access to "Dummies®" books yet. We don't know for sure, but it probably went something like this: Mommy was approaching his baby crib. Mommy had her legs moving and the crib had wheels. Was Mommy moving toward him, or was the crib moving toward her

on its wheels, like people sitting in moving carriages? Keep in mind --
the year was 1880. Einstein didn't even have words for the concept of
relative movement -- didn't need it. The important thing was, Mommy
was getting much, much closer!

It took baby Albert another 26 years to cross all the t's and dot all
the i's, but remember, all of society was conspiring to dumb this kid
down.

Now take Einstein's grasp of the importance of variable time, as
opposed to fixed and absolute time: Here's where dumbing down really
gets serious. Not only did Einstein have to overcome all the incorrect
learning that had been rammed into his young head, but he also had to
overcome all the kvetchiness inherent in the German language. I don't
mean to insult the German language speakers, but don't they always
sound like they're complaining about something? Take Gutten Nacht,
for good night. Does that sound good? It sounds to me like the person
needs to clear his throat. But Einstein already had some pretty sound
ideas about fixed time (meaning everybody everywhere has the same
time) versus variable time.

I know something about variable time. Variable time is the way I
keep most of my appointments, whereas my husband uses a fixed time
system, after first checking with the U.S. Naval Observatory. Moving
on here, Einstein, as a baby, had no difficulties dealing with time -- he
had no difficulty recognizing when it was time to eat, time to pee, time
to exercise, time to sleep, etc. There was nothing absolute about when
things needed to happen -- when he had to go, he went. If he would
have spoken at one year, he'd have told Mommy, "Hey, don't bother
me now; I'm thinking about how to escape this cage you've got me
in." Or something along those lines. Of course, Mommy had already
been dumbed down by custom and would have had to look at her own

timepiece to figure out when it was time for her to feed little Albert. Her time was most likely different from his time.

There is no such thing as absolute time and every little baby knows it. But don't tell this to my husband -- he looks at his watch to decide if he's hungry or sleepy.

Incidentally, I do not claim to understand this time thing at all. I'm just making an obvious point that babies keep things simple and don't start screwing around with our minds until they get a little bigger and start attending school. Also, I don't really understand the Theory of Special or General Relativity either. I just know about my relatives, and they all believe that I waste a lot of my time. My own children, who live in another time zone from me, can't even figure out how to get me on any kind of a phone, cell or otherwise. I'm waiting for the next brilliant inventor to figure out how my kids can reach me when they need to, without getting totally pissed off

Now back to my little crude cartoon at the beginning of this chapter: It illustrates my theory that a really smart baby can come out with a major scientific breakthrough if he or she can cut out all the adult nonsense that gets in the way before the math is worked out.

Now here's more on the intelligence issue, even though if I hadn't been dumbed down, I would have provided less, or maybe even eliminated the whole damned subject.

I'm going to go back to Einstein because he's such a good example of a human avoiding most of the dumbing down. Einstein had to learn mathematics after he learned physics to prove what he already knew. I'm not insulting mathematics experts. We need them. Physicists are especially useful. There are things humans can't see, like atoms and quarks and their cousins and other progeny. It's hard to admit, but I think physicists and mathematicians are even more useful than lawyers. They come up with ideas that make our lives way more fun. Take, for example, the teeny tiny thing that makes your IPOD® work. Lawyers don't make anything more fun -- they screw it all up and make a living doing it. I'm a tax lawyer myself, so I know what I'm talking about. I tell people how much they have to pay the Government. I know that's no fun for them, so I try to entertain them, while I'm really screwing up all their plans. I think I should have been a physicist, but I was scared off by a really rude high school geometry teacher who didn't recognize my potential. I hid in a hole after that course whenever the opportunity arose for me to take more math. Today, I realize that my jealousy over the kids who braved advanced math and physics courses turned me into a lawyer.

I just realized that somebody reading this (if I should live so long and be so lucky) might have been offended at my characterization of the German language. Well, don't sweat it. I have other stuff up my sleeve for the Italians, the French and the Slavic people too. Actually, Americans are my very favorite target. They are so very naive about everything, especially improving health and hunger in the World. Well, who started McDonald's®? It wasn't a chap from Somali.

When I was about three years old I discovered books. My parents didn't own books, but somebody finally gave me a book. I knew it was something to distract me from destroying the furniture, but who cares? Then I found out about public libraries. I wasn't allowed in our local Public Library because its keeper thought that I wouldn't be able to keep quiet. I don't know where that person got that idea from -- I would have done anything, maybe even put a lid on my mouth, to mess with all those great books. I would probably even have gone so far as to deposit my chocolate candy in a receptacle at the door. Well, maybe I would have just stuffed it in my pocket somewhere.

Then I went on to reading beginners' books. I read a sentence -- "See Dick run. See Jane cry," etc. Why the hell did Dick run and

Jane cry? I privately believed that Jane should have done the running with Dick doing the crying. After I had completely absorbed Dick and Jane, I went on to read about animals. This reading stage happened prior to humans becoming nicer to animals. All the animals I read about suffered. Black Beauty© went from owner to owner and suffered feelings of loss. Sounds like me with my babysitter turnover. Lassie© came home filthy and wiped out. Bambi's© mother got plugged and his father kicked the bucket soon after. Finally, I read a book about an animal that didn't suffer so much -- Dumbo the Elephant©. Did you know that was originally a book? Dumbo finally conquered the real Fear of Flying. (See my chapter about my retirement.) This was a really happy ending for a large animal. Life was definitely not all bad for animals, so I finally discovered.

There was hope for me after all.

CHAPTER SEVEN
THE TRUTH ABOUT MY
RETIREMENT

If you have time to read this, you probably are not retired

I get nervous when I think about having retirement leisure. The word "retirement" scares me so much that I need to take a vacation to relieve the stress. It's probably because in my head I'm still back in college, having suffered incomplete matriculation syndrome. This malady cannot be cured by retiring, since the only way to recover is to succeed in the field of one's original major, whether or not it's a good idea. To me, that sounds a lot like hard work, and hard work is the antithesis of retirement. Some retirees I have met would disagree with this. How many times have you heard a retired guy tell you that since retiring, he is busier than ever? I've heard it a lot. Whenever I encounter that situation, I scratch my head and think to myself, "How nuts is that?" So I've concluded that I can never retire because I'm just too darned lazy.

When I look around me in sunny south Florida, I get shpilkies just realizing that all these "Over-55" communities have a lot of people living in them that are even younger than me. It's enough of a wake-up call at my age to turn the roots of my hair from medium gray to light gray -- that is, if you could find my roots underneath all the latest color formula. I let my hairdresser deal with my roots, while I sit in his chair, innocently pretending that I'm being an honest woman, never guilty of trying to fool Mother Nature. I have a similar attitude when the eyebrow waxing lady does her best to eliminate my John L. Lewis look, which would alter my facial expression if left on its own.

I know that I have always resisted each approaching birthday and wished I were younger than I was about to become. I had so much grief when I was only five years old, that I sometimes wanted to go back and get born all over again. Are there any "born again" Jewish people out there? Let me know, because I have not only gotten older, I have begun to lose things, like all my Jewish books. The only one I can still find is a wrinkled paperback copy of Jennie Grossinger's cookbook, written back in the late fifties, based on recipes she developed as a matriarch of the no longer standing Grossinger's Resort in the Catskills. At least I haven't lost the Catskills -- I lived in their foothills for over ten years, and, to my knowledge, they are still standing there, exactly where I left them.

Speaking of books, I go crazy looking for books I don't seem to have any longer. I've never disposed of a book, but somebody has, because many of them are gone. The other day I was looking for a copy of Leo Rosten's book about Jewish idioms -- see, I can't even remember the title of it -- and it wasn't anywhere in my house. I have about six different bookcases, not counting the two in the humid garage, and then the seventeen shelves that are scattered around the place, in my home office, in my bedroom, even a couple in the toilet area that has been made into sort of a hygiene library. I looked in all of them. No Leo Rosten, damn, not anywhere. Then I remembered the two libraries I had stashed under the beds, so I looked there also. That was a big problem, getting down on all fours and feeling sickly upon observing all the dust bunnies and expired Floridian insect life. Not only didn't I find the literary object of my search, I had to get up again and attempt to stand up straight without exclaiming "Oy." Did I ask for this pain and suffering with not even anybody to sue?

Everybody tells me I should be grateful for my good health. My response is, the doctors should be grateful -- the longer I live to have all the tests they dish out, the more of my co-payments they get to pocket to expend on new golf gear and trips to India. Yes, I'm grateful, but I'm grateful with a hook. Call it an asterisk, if you prefer. The footnote relating to my use of the term "grateful" should state: "A state of being thankful for all blessings you have when what you really want is more value in your 401(k) and fewer wrinkles." So yes, I'm grateful that I can still express myself, even if I'm a teeny bit sulky. I'm not as sulky as my ancestors, however. Now there's a family clan who really had the corner on sulking. I remember my bubby in her kitchen with the green icebox and the single bottle of prune juice in it -- one of her favorite sulks was, "Vy did Got gif me such a life, and vy didn't efen von of my kids come to the cemetery ven Hymie vas laid there -- and vy iss my mondel bread not finished yet, maybe even before dey haf to lay me out in the ground there? Vy, oh vy?"

When it comes to sulking, I consider it a complete waste of negative karma. I do something else when I am in a bad mood -- I mutter to the computer, or sometimes curse at one of the alleged non-stick pots in my kitchen, or, if I am really ticked off, I might get off a mild rant in a Letter to some Editor. Then I try to give thanks that I still remember enough of the English language to express my anger and enough sense to keep my mouth shut without getting arrested for disturbing the peace. I feel grateful that my grandmother, of whom I was very fond, taught me some good values. It's better to sulk than to offend someone who has the power to force you to spend entire days with good weather stuck in some courtroom, trying to fix the problem.

There is a dim memory (actually most of my memories are pretty dim) which I have that teaches people of the Jewish faith to give thanks for all the blessings bestowed upon us and to celebrate a lot. They even made up a bunch of new holidays to do it in. Now if only I could find some of those books -- especially the ones that tell you how they decide when the holidays are.

I know I'm not a bad person because I have mended my ways and learned to clean out the jars before I recycle. Also, I have kindly thoughts toward all of my old friends, even the ones to whom I no longer speak because I have lost their addresses and phone numbers. Once in awhile an old friend pops up, having searched the e-mail directory, and found me, even tracing my movements through three different States. There was a sweet classmate of mine (younger than me, of course) who found me via an Internet search. I gave her a lot of credit because I'm difficult to find when my acting out type of existence is similar to that of a groundhog. Let me explain -- I have my own type of hole to duck into. My husband refers to it as the one in my head, but my description is much kinder -- I call it "failure to communicate." What that means is that I forget to check my cell phone, I neglect to check my land line phone messages promptly, and I can't always find the current day's mail, which winds up under my obsolete laptop. You might think, "Well, thank goodness there is e-mail!" I was afraid you were going to think that. Here's the scoop: I check my e-mail only when I'm a little bit constipated, because my desktop computer on my desk (and where else would a desktop computer be?) is very conveniently located near our second bathroom. I really don't want to say any more on this subject.

I was talking about my memory and my sulking and, originally, why I am afraid to face retirement. Let's start with my memory:

1. <u>My Memory</u>. I've decided to skip this area for now and go back to it later, i.e., if I remember to do it;

2. <u>Fear of Retirement.</u> Erica Jong wrote a book entitled "Fear of Flying©." It wasn't about aviation, however, it was about having a good time, I believe. I liked the title because it was so very misleading. I thought it was an incredible promotional idea to name a book in such a way that some people would buy it and put it on a credit card before realizing that it wasn't about aviation. I realize that many people will crack open a book prior to purchase, giggle at the pictures, if there are any amusing ones, and then ensconce in some chair at one of the surviving big box bookstore chains. Of course they will then leave the book on the unpaid-for book table, having gotten what they came for. Anyway, I would still like to use this approach and name a book of mine about retirement "Fear of Mah JJongh." Then, maybe, persons in a hurry, who really wanted to learn about Mah JJongh, might accidentally buy the book, thinking that it would help them conquer

their fear. I asked my husband what he thought of that idea, and he didn't answer me, even though we had made eye contact. He does that when my questions don't merit a vocal answer, which, I have to confess, is most of the time.

Now, getting back to Fear of Retirement, certain points need to be addressed, at least before you or your over-the-shoulder stalker, throw down this mush I've written prior to your even finding your way to the free book reading table. Incidentally, did you know the reason bookstore personnel have to have, among other requirements, strong backs? Yes, it's true, whether you notice or not, they are always picking up hastily flung books off the floor. I might add that this book-flinging syndrome evident in big box bookstores is dwarfed by clothing-flinging patrons at big box discount retailers everywhere. Why we have become a nation of flingers when we used to be a nation of mere polite gawkers and appreciaters is somewhat of a mystery to me. I think it happened when "self service" store trends arrived and people who were not very skilled at reading thought it meant "selfish service." Oh why oh why do I lament so? Can't we all just get along?

I am afraid of retirement because retirement is for people who think they have saved enough money to stop working for money. Some people can retire on multiple government pensions, I have heard, and are referred to as triple-dippers. I'm not talking about politicians, however, who comprise a totally different species altogether. I refer to their species as "homo electus." They're the only living creatures other than kangaroos who walk around with their futures in their pockets.

I wish I had been a triple dipping civil servant. The only Government service I have engaged in is the indirect kind when I help one of our rotating mail carriers by directing my neighbors' letters to their actual addresses instead of in my own mailbox. My mailbox is the Government's official receptacle for what I call solicitations plus. I added the word, "plus" for the few times I receive an actual piece of mail which is neither bulk advertising nor other unrequested information paid for by a lot of unsuspecting taxpayers.

I know that I have not saved enough money for retirement for two reasons: (1) I save low, and (2) I live high. Other than that, I might be able to accumulate sufficient investments some day to take a few weeks off, and that is on the condition that I go on an extremely strict diet and don't, for God's sake, try to drive anywhere. But some people I know think they can retire in comfort and actually do give the old boss the heave-ho. I found out that a couple I knew who were living in the most expensive home in our community were having trouble keeping up with their expenses, and, short of either of them going back to drudge work, were now bombarding my mailbox with literature about their new venture. This venture was expressly designed to enable them to sit back and enjoy life under a palm tree while a bunch of us other suckers did all their business for them. I admired them for their moxie and even went to a meeting, where I was frightened by the prospect of taking up this venture because it would require using e-mails EVERY SINGLE DAY. That was enough to send me packing.

I have more problems with the prospect of retirement than I have already alluded to. Let's say I have an appointment with a new type of doctor, which has become a regular thing with me. That's because I still haven't been diagnosed with any of the extremely terminal diseases yet. I have been taught by my deceased ancestors to bite my tongue when I speak of this. Repeated bouts of my biting my tongue over the years are now resulting in some tissue damage. This could be cause for alarm, for I might have to visit a mouth doctor. Is there such a thing? There has to be. There is a subspecialty for every malady today. It must belong to the "Eye, Ear, Nose and Throat" gang, but I haven't actually checked that out. Well, let's go hypothetical. Suppose that you go to the mouth doctor when you have an issue with any portion of your mouth, other than with your teeth or an unattractive lip pucker, but which definitely would include any tongue maladies. The type of injury resulting from biting your tongue seems to be more prevalent among Jewish people, but I'm not really sure of my facts.

Maybe you have a different kind of mouth injury. Perhaps you got socked in the jaw, in which case you might have to see more than one doctor because of the multiple problems a sock in the jaw might involve. I can think of at least four different specialists who would want to put you on their patient recall lists after the afore-mentioned jaw injury. You never want to cross the line and see the wrong doctor, because you will have to pay the wrong one for taking up appointment time, and then find out who the right one was and then pay that one. Then, at each of the multiplicity of initial visits, you must fill out a ten-page form, single-spaced, with very small type, barely readable because it has been duplicated so many times using the cheapest equipment on the planet. One of the blanks they want you to fill in is "Occupation." I would not even dare to put the word "retired" on that line. It will simply give that medical office leave to think up more tests for me as a subcategory of patients who are tactfully referred to as "elderly." So I'm very careful when I get to that line -- I put down "Retail Store Slave." No one has ever questioned me about that because they already have my medical insurance card and they can now legally invade my privacy and discover I am telling the truth.

I know the word "slave" is a dicey word to use because it has gotten a very bad rap from certain groups who have suffered discrimination. I want to make it perfectly clear right up front that I Never Discriminate. I offend everybody -- and I do it equally. However, because I don't want to be roped into signing up for a course on Sensitivity, I have considered using a synonym for the word "slave." Possibilities are: "grunt", "menial laborer", "unskilled worker", or "trainee".

I have actually been a trainee my entire life, because, no matter what job I have had, every day at work I learn something new. Yesterday I learned that another trainee at my current job, whom I personally trained, was now my boss. These things don't upset me because when promotional opportunities are posted on the bulletin board, I read the job description. If it reads more than four lines, I think, "No way." Then I continue walking toward the restroom, which is just past the bulletin board.

In conclusion, because I don't have to write "retired" on the applicable line of the doctor's poop sheet, I don't have to wait very long in the waiting room prior to being called by a squeaky-voiced woman in medical garb and then ushered into the coldest possible room they have where you notice that the most comfortable seat is the cot with the stirrups. Usually, that's a long wait, interrupted only by the excitement of the entry of a cleaning person who needs to empty the trash can of stuff you don't want to know about. Still, by not being "retired," I get to skip the even longer wait in the ante room, followed by the now familiar long wait in the aforesaid cold room. Why is this true? My guess is that when they think you are retired, they sense that you don't have a job to go to and they can juggle you around more. It is possible I may have made all this up, but what can you expect from a senior citizen who has spent so much time watching CNN® in doctors' waiting rooms?

Here's another problem about retirement: what if I decide that I want to be an unemployed writer on a full-time basis? What if my husband and I are sitting next to each other on the sofa and he suddenly feels romantic? He might even want to reach over and hold my hand, which is jiggling a ballpoint pen scribbling away with a bubbling great idea? Knowing him as I do, he'll get quickly turned off, thinking, "foiled again, by a Bic," and then retreat into his normal introspective persona. These are serious matters. I'm better off having him pine after me while I'm working my day job.

As I look over what I have just laid out, in a disorganized kind of way, I feel that the arguments I have made for not retiring are somewhat incomplete. Then again, I probably will be in the middle of contemplating the wisdom of it when there will be a sudden phone call from one of my kids excitedly announcing to me that something amazing has happened! My kid has decided that it's time to retire! Not only that, but some of the funds to make it possible will be coming from me in the form of a future inheritance! If there's one thing I cannot tolerate, it's the prospect of having one of my kids upstage me like that. If my kid told me a thing like that, do you think I will be sending any more gift cards when birthday time comes around? What if my kid uses the gift card money to buy a hammock? Or even worse, an island cruise? Doesn't sound like a plan I could endorse with much enthusiasm. It would be a race between us to the nearest travel agent specializing in senior tours.

That being said, I think I'll just continue working for awhile and maybe have my phone disconnected and change my e-mail address.

Naaaahhh!

CHAPTER EIGHT
THE TRUTH ABOUT MY
CONGEVITY

Nobody knows how long an already old person has left, so it might be a good idea to check the local Bureau of Vital Statistics before sending any birthday presents

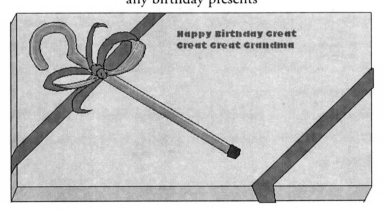

I know that I'm going to live to be one hundred and ten.[2] That's going to be my punishment for being exceptionally lazy and uptight about my figure. It also means I'm going to have 39 more birthdays where I can't really eat much cake. No one who still hangs out in my circles will know what to get me for a present that I don't already have

---

[2] If I'm dead by the time you read this, check the Internet for where to send the donations in lieu of flowers

five of. I'm not even going to be in a wheelchair because right now they are inventing something that will have me vaulting around the house on artificial limbs. I feel sorry for those poor souls who may have to pay for all this stuff. However, I'm going to be selfish and stay alive, just to get back at all the doctors who will not have believed that I would make it this far because I never had all their prescriptions filled.

If any of my three kids is still around and breathing, then that kid will be at least 80 years old and still waiting for the little bit I've got left. Since I will probably figure out how to curtail my spending by then, I should have quite a bit of compounded interest building up in my bank accounts. Or maybe they'll call them credits, or some such method of keeping track of my wealth. I will also have written another 39 books, either entirely unpublished, or self-published at somebody else's expense. My longevity will be my revenge against those do-gooder types who decided that someone as old as I am needed help. The way things are going now, that help will definitely come from some people who didn't want to be bothered.

This is not a gloomy outlook. It's scary. There's a whole plot out there to keep me alive so that I can continue to suffer every time the economy goes into the tank, forcing me to come up with new schemes to beat those speculating gamers. English will no longer be spoken, naturally, because I won't be a plain vanilla American any longer. I will be referred to as a Kurdistanian-American. The World as we know it will be three quarters Euromuslimamerind and one quarter Turkisfranconian. It pisses me off that I will have had to learn two more languages, but there will be special atomitronic translators installed into a portion of my brain so that I can just brush up on each dialect in thirty seconds. Nobody will dare harm an artificial hair on my smooth head because my life will have been grandfathered in by the alumni of the Lawyers' Platoon.

I don't really care. So what if I'm just a relic of the outdated feminist fizzle. I won't need causes or activism to keep me occupied because I'll be spending most of my time playing Rap Bach on my Spinadoodle Chord-Making Device. The neighbors will have put mute buttons on their domicile barriers so that they don't have to hear it and the non-endangered rhinocerosimian crawling creature will be my service animal. I will have been awarded the use of this creature for free because I was the winner of the name-a-codfish-baby contest. My winning entry explained in one of the new languages what I would do to protect this variety of fish baby so that it could continue to display its feelings without fear of being branded or tagged.

I think it will be very interesting to be this old because I will probably still be working on trying to act my age. I can actually visualize being in that time frame. Wow! I'm There!

Thank you very much for your courtesy during this interview, and please shut my igloo door when you leave, because that fifty below weather outside is a bit chilly for my old bones. Too bad that Global Warming thing really crapped out on us -- big time.

CHAPTER NINE
THE TRUTH ABOUT MY
POLITICAL AMBITIONS

(You may not want to use the following as a model for your own
aspirations)

I don't know if I can write the following summarization of my
political ambitions effectively because I have almost always lied to
myself about my leadership skills. I might be lying right now.

I have known people who listened attentively to some ideas I've shared and all that I had to say, only to notice that these same people, after my talk, saw me in the street and passed me by in their cars while I was limping down the road -- and this was in a rainstorm.

If I want to get my message across, I have to Fed-Ex® it in a large Pak bearing the return address of a local police department. Otherwise it would go in the junk mail pile.

I've planned social gatherings at my house, including sending out cleverly worded invitations, only to wind up eating most of the leftover food earmarked for no-shows. To add insult to injury, I have gotten sick later that night and wound up puking for several hours.

I hardly ever have my doorbell rung by trick or treaters on Halloween night, even when the weather is superb, and I have advertised that I give out large portions.

I'm so forgettable that I've even thought about feigning a sex scandal involving myself and a mythical rich uncle, or, alternatively, a couple of female judges. The catch is that someone would have to help me get a press release about it in the newspaper on a slow news day, and even then, it would probably be buried somewhere as a 3-liner in the section where they list errors and corrections, or even worse, in the public legal notice section.

Here's my biggest gripe: My ISP, my very own server, will simply not remember me, no matter how many times I check the box "Remember me on this computer." I know that if I try to contact my server, to which I pay lots of dollars every month via automatic billing, I will get another message which further assures me I am a non-person according to their records. So I keep checking that "remember" box, even though I have thoughts about saving a few mouse clicks and stifling my emotions.

I've concluded that I'm just not a big draw.

So, even though I'd probably be an excellent state senator, I suspect I'd have trouble getting enough people in my district to sign my petition without handing out valuable gift certificates. Some of the signers of my petition would probably do it on the condition that I attend a relative's time-share presentation 200 miles away.

I don't like to think of myself as a loser, so I take tranquilizing medications when I'm not even depressed.

Woody Allen is my all-time hero with his bumbling persona, and I sent a fan letter to him telling him so, which got returned for lack of postage. Also, the returned envelope, which contained my picture, was hopelessly mangled. It got returned to the wrong house, and the only way I found out about it was to notice it in the neighbor's stack of yard refuse.

I decided to take a public speaking and presentation class, which also included singing lessons, and practice my skills at home. Then I noticed that there were no more birds in the trees on my property. My husband walks around with earplugs anyway, but during my practice lessons, I couldn't find him. Then I discovered that he had been going to Home Depot® to research how much it would cost to soundproof his private computer closet.

I have spent thousands of dollars on the kind of therapy that is designed to have me better connect with people and manage my anger. Every time I got a bill for a month's sessions, I got so mad that I would go outside and tear lawn grass out by its roots. Then I got a nasty letter from my homeowner's association about the ugly holes in my lawn. I showed up at the landscape committee to plead my case and got into a fight with a ninety-two year old woman. I lost. Even though I decided to spend even more on those therapy sessions, I was informed by them that new enrollment had been suspended because they were full. I complained that I wasn't a new applicant. They had never heard of me.

I could go on and on, but I don't want to get into the bad news.

Yes, I've concluded that I probably should have begun my path to the Presidency of the United States when I had the chance, right after the Vietnam War. I had no money, no connections, no self-confidence, no political program, no grass root supporters, and no sense of follow-through. But I did have one great idea, which would have saved the United States a lot of grief. This idea was not only super; it was way ahead of its time. I had typed it very carefully, edited it with the skill of the combined staff of Random House, and made multiple copies. Unfortunately, I don't know where I put it. "So what", you say, "What was your great idea?" I'm afraid I can't answer that. I sort of forgot exactly what it was. I think it had something to do with tearing down a wall, somewhere, I think in some country in Africa.

So, in conclusion, I think you should vote for me, whenever I get my organization together again.

CHAPTER TEN
THE TRUTH ABOUT MY
"HAVING IT ALL"

Every story needs some kind of a conclusion -- otherwise a reader will get to the last page and think, "Was that the end of it? Did the butler really do it, or was it the sanitation worker?"

I never completed my Journalism training, which I began at Northwestern University, nor my Fiction Writing program, which I started at Columbia College in Chicago. So, since I have promised to tell the truth about a lot of things, I am not sure how to end anything. All my life has been about beginnings.

But I will put in this conclusion that will perhaps satisfy anyone who took the trouble to read this whole collection of anecdotal mutterings: Yes, this is the last of it in this book, and the reader can finish it and put it wherever finished books are put. My husband puts most of his finished books in the floor of our garage, ready for waste pickup. He claims that we have no more room in our house for books. I, however, can still see space for additional shelves higher up on the walls because we have higher than average ceilings. However, I am a short person and a klutz with a hammer and nails, and, especially with an electric drill. So I have to hide any books which I intend to keep and I am, really, running out of room.

I didn't mean to sound like I am complaining because I really do "have it all." I started out wanting to have the Sun and the Moon and the Stars, and by gosh, I have them. I wanted to be a writer, and whoopee do, I not only wrote something, I am offering it to you and you and you.

This writing is just my slant on a bunch of things that concern me. Now, go see if you can return this book and get your money back. Or be like me -- find another shelf in some part of your abode where you can have it until you have to move or they take you away.

Good luck.

This is   THE END.

LaVergne, TN USA
17 September 2009
158229LV00003B/7/P